Authentic Motivation in Schools

Authentic Motivation in Schools

A treatise on motivation and
the modern education system

special thanks...

...to the pioneers who would all be told they're wrong.

Contents

Preface

"To myself I am only a child playing on the beach, while vast oceans of truth lie undiscovered before me."

—Issac Newton

When I searched for a simple, accurate book that focused on the topic of motivation—as it relates to schooling—I couldn't find what I was looking for. My plan was to purchase as many copies of this book that I could afford, and give them away to fellow educators. I desperately wanted this book to exist. But while there is literature on "motivation and learning" within the field of educational psychology, and there are various education books on the topic, I never found the right book to stock.

Don't get me wrong. Alfie Kohn's "Punished by Rewards" is an incredible book. By its end, the traditional school and classroom are seen for what they are: heavily flawed, and ultimately outdated. The "traditional" system is not just torn down, either. A greater foundation is offered in place of the old way.

If every educator read and understood *Punished by Rewards*, I believe that would change everything. The problem, I realized, is that that will not happen. One reason why is because the book is not a quick and easy read, and the tone is often confrontational. While I personally enjoyed it, and set aside the time and energy to read it, I understood that this book would not appeal to some of the people it most needed to reach.

A few years later, I read "Drive" by Dan Pink. This book was less dense than Punished by Rewards, less contrarian (but still contrarian enough), and more of a "fun" read. Maybe this is the book I should give to educators everywhere?

But the problem here is that Dan Pink's major focus is on the workplace. Though he does include some discussion of education, including many of the problems and some possible solutions, Dan Pink does not have experience as a teacher, nor is he primarily focused on education.

Of course, there are many books out there I haven't read, or simply don't know about. But I flipped through a lot of the ones on motivation, and I just couldn't find the right book!

It turns out, I was looking for a very specific book. I eventually realized that the book I was looking for was already sketched out in my mind. I spent years in research, conversation, observation, and some practice, too, learning about new education concepts. And I wanted to distill the greatness of the thought leaders, so that these ideas would be easily accessible, highly relevant, and hopefully fun to read. I couldn't let it go. There was a niche that I thought needed me. I took the advice that prompted my last book. *If the book you want to read doesn't exist, it's your job to write it.*

—

As a substitute teacher for several years, I had the chance to observe students outside their natural habitat and normal classroom procedures. This gave me a unique perspective on their motivation. If students desperately avoid doing their assignment when the regular teacher is gone, for example, what does that say about their motivation? And what does it say, perhaps, about the assignment and its motivational value?

Some classes have more than one teacher, and occasionally I would sub for one of these "co-teachers." During this time, I had the chance to watch many teachers teach their classes. I spent time in conversation with teachers and administrators, and often steered the talk toward student motivation.

I spoke with students as well, to get their perspective.

I did this in more than twenty schools around the district—some for a day, some for a year, and the rest in-between. I was on a mission. I wanted to understand "the system."

What I found was a lot of teachers talking about motivation, and very concerned with it—but rarely, if ever, a mention of the modifiers "intrinsic" or "extrinsic."

I found that teachers did not appear to structure their classrooms and lessons around the implications of different "kinds" of motivation. Specifically, that these different "types" of motivation are not merely two subsets of the same thing, but different altogether, and that these different kinds of "motivation" actually work to defeat each other, not simply add to each other. I felt that, if this were truly understood, schools and classrooms would look very different than how they do look, and educators would be using an entirely different set of words and actions.

This is not a calling out of teachers, and teachers alone. That was never my goal. I simply believed, and would confirm, that this is a traditional way of teaching, and a cultural phenomenon. "Extrinsic" strategies are mainstay pedagogical tools which are thought to be productive and constructive. It is what teachers are taught, told, and expected to do.

The way to "motivate" people by using punishments and rewards, however, is a kind of cultural mythology or persistent pseudo-wisdom. Despite the constant rhetoric everywhere that we do "what's best" for the students, the way we "motivate" learners in schools is certainly not what's "best," and this is not just an opinion, it is backed by quite a bit of research and solid arguments by now.

Alfie Kohn has been writing, researching, and speaking about education-related motivation for many years. He writes:

"Many teachers, I find, are familiar with the modifiers "intrinsic" and "extrinsic," yet they continue to talk about "how motivated" a student is or how to "motivate" kids in general. By overlooking the critical difference between types of motivation, they contribute to a serious problem."[1]

Yes, a *serious problem*, that is constantly under the radar. I figured it was true that many teachers, if not most, have heard the terms "intrinsic and "extrinsic" motivation, and many have done more than simply heard the terms. Teachers often have a general idea of what these terms mean, from their study in teacher-education programs. It is not difficult to believe that this basic difference is covered, or at least mentioned, in teacher training. I vaguely recall the terms in my own program. We had an occasional discussion about "motivation," with fleeting and shallow mentions of "intrinsic" and "extrinsic." It was not a major topic of study—like it should be —but it was there.

Being familiar with the terms on a basic level does not mean a fundamental understanding of the concept—or the implications for teaching and learning. Where I suspect most teachers (and virtually everyone else) fall short is that we do not systemically understand that while we *want* students to be intrinsically-motivated, and we *ask* (beg) students to be intrinsically-motivated, at the same time we *train* them to be extrinsically-motivated.

We implicitly teach students that "extrinsic motivation" is the way: it's how you do school, it's how you will do your job in the future, it's how you get through life and make your way in the world. We tell them to have their own reasons, and to live and learn for those reasons—but we also tell them the opposite. You must live, work, and learn primarily because other people told you, bribed you, and ultimately "made" you.

This is a summary of the problem. Take a system-view and imagine our school system as one person, and this one person would not understand that "intrinsic" motivation is qualitatively different from "extrinsic" motivation, and that they act as opposing forces.

Extrinsic and intrinsic motivation are not simply different ways to achieve the same goal. They are not simply "reinforcing" of one another. And for educators, they call for different approaches, which lead to different results. By "results" I mean "who the students become," and that's why we have such a responsibility to get it right.

We want the students to "try harder," "challenge yourself," "do your best," "love to learn," and on and on. But the structures of school, and our toolbox of practices as parents, educators, and administrators make it very difficult for the students to feel this way and do these things. If students are constantly told, for example, that grades matter a lot, and they *are* told this constantly, then it is only logical for those students to choose the easier task and stay within the defined expectation of whoever set the requirements. The more a student challenges oneself—and tries to do more than what was explicitly asked—the less likely this student will receive a good grade. By trying something more difficult, the student might miss a deadline. The student might make more mistakes. The student might get the "wrong" answers, or come up with no answer at all. In such a strict evaluative environment, based on fulfilling someone else's expectations, it is certainly *possible* to go beyond expectations—but it is not "safe" to do so, and therefore, is irrational to the student.

That, not "human nature," is an illustration of why so many students insist on coloring in the lines, and moving only when we tell them. The student knows, because we continually tell her, that if she does something more difficult or different from the norm, she will less likely get something good in return. By venturing outside the instructions and specific criteria, this student could get a lower class rank; maybe won't get that scholarship; won't get the special award; won't be praised by friends, teachers, and family; won't go to a college that is "good enough" (or won't go at all);

won't get as good of a job—basically, will have a worse life. That is the threat/promise, at least. It is reasonable and "wise" for the students to heed this threat/promise, and we tell them frequently that they must take our threats and promises seriously.

Our approach of extrinsic motivation thus shapes the students' idea of learning into *"what do I have to do to be approved?"* rather than *"what can or should I ultimately do, in my own view?"* The students learn that others will think for them and initiate most things for them. Maybe they will break this habit, eventually, but it certainly *is* a habit they develop—and certainly, many *will not* break the habit later in life, and we cannot count on them to break it later in life.

Many teachers recognize this truth. It is a great challenge, and persistent teacher complaint, to "motivate" students into thinking more deeply and taking initiative. But the flat student response to this persistent effort of parents and educators is not just a matter of being lazy, being a kid, or refusing our personal requests. It's a matter of their structural environment and learning conditions, and how they've been trained to game the system—"passing" through the endless requirements while minimizing the stress on themselves.

The students lose their sense of initiative for many reasons, but a major one is that we grade and score the students according to how well they align with the uniform and arbitrary "standards." These standards come from the state, the department chair, teachers, or wherever—usually some combination thereof—and the idea is that anyone and everyone aside from the students themselves will determine what the students are "supposed" to learn, how they will learn, when they will learn, and even why they will learn. Then, the students are punished or rewarded according to their "success" in meeting someone else's instructions and expectations.

It's safe to say that this approach de-motivates human beings in that it diminishes their intrinsic spirit to learn, and so they must continually be enticed by external elements. When the superficial enticements stop, the students stop. And that is what so much research has found, and yet, the research and basic concept are ignored.

We kick the can down the road. We use threats, bribes, and punishments to get them working. This approach consistently lowers the chance that students will find the curriculum interesting for its own sake. Now "learning" is just something they have to do to get something else, or to avoid something unpleasant to themselves.

Things like grades, which are extrinsic motivators, do matter. They do not matter in a "universal" or natural sense—they do not matter like water *matters*, or friendship *matters*—they matter in that we place an incredible social value on them. Grades are essentially an educational fad in this place and time. Educators talk about lots of ridiculous fads in education, and I often agree, but what about grades? They were not the past, they are not eternally present, and they are not the future. Grades are merely a fad because grades are not a *necessity* for learning, or even for evaluation, and they do actual harm to the learning process and the learners themselves.

But, grades are simply the best example of "extrinsic" motivators. There are many, almost endlessly, more. I will help you learn to see them, all around you—and what this kind of environment means for teaching and learning. And some ideas for challenging and changing it.

—

"The problem isn't with kids' attitudes or motivation as much as it is with our policies and practices." [2]
-Alfie Kohn

The problem with students, if we are to generalize, is not *childhood*, or "being a teenager," as is oft assumed or implied when addressing problems of motivation in school. The problem lies much more in our beliefs and institutions. If we acknowledge this, we are then forced to ask a different set of questions in approaching problems of motivation. To improve our policies and practices, we would not begin with the question: *"How do we fix our kids' failure to conform and behave?"*, but instead, *"How do we fix our ideas and expectations about students, school, and learning?"*

After asking the right questions, we can proceed in coming up with correct policy and practice. If we're serious about improving the school experience for students, and giving them a better education (which is closely tied with the former), we adopt the view of changing the system rather than trying to "fix" each individual kid. The students don't need to be fixed. Their environment does.

We've done it wrong for far too long. Most of what I argue and illustrate in this book has already been said elsewhere, in some form, and I often refer to the two motivation experts Alfie Kohn and Dan Pink. But this book is ultimately my own work and my own view. As I draw from others throughout this book, it's done in order to support my own observations and experience as a professional educator. Despite all the existing material on motivation, I felt this book was necessary to write. Otherwise, I wouldn't have written it. I would have simply bought copies of a book that already existed, and given them away to everyone I could.

I think most serious parents and educators already do believe that we should teach people to love learning, think for themselves, care about others, and seek challenge rather than avoid it. But if we want *that*... then why are we doing *this*? Or, if we want intrinsically-motivated students, why do we persist in doing so much that undermines their intrinsic motivation?

Fortunately, these problems are not stuck in stone, and we already have some great knowledge and principles for guiding the way forward. It wouldn't be an easy or straightforward path to "motivational" schools and classrooms, but we don't have to re-invent or discover so many new ideas. It's already there, waiting to be acknowledged. The truth is that school doesn't simply need little tweaks, "higher standards," or more treats for the kiddos. It needs to be built on a better foundation, and a major plank of that foundation would be a sounder concept of motivation.

Introduction

"A lack of engagement is the main reason for the challenges that teachers face in schools and classrooms today."[3]

—Pasi Sahlberg

Pasi Sahlberg is former Director General at the Finnish Ministry of Education, and holds other impressive credentials (among them the education best-seller *Finnish Lessons 2.0: What can the world learn from educational change in Finland?*"). Sahlberg has examined schools, classrooms, and political systems around the world as they relate to education systems. He's more experienced than me as an educator, holds a PhD, and is way more famous. And here's what he wrote: "a lack of engagement" is *the number one problem teachers face*.

I imagine many teachers would agree. I have frequently watched the struggle of teachers in their classrooms, often noting their exasperation and hopelessness at the end of class. I have listened to the ranting in the teacher's lounge and the disciplinary office; the frustration at the end of the school day; the "good grief" and sighs of relief on holiday breaks and weekends. And I have experienced it myself, (though not as much as some who have been doing it for many decades).

Somehow I feel that if students were not lacking in engagement, teachers' lives would be easier. And more than that, students would learn better.

In Sahlberg's quote about a lack of student engagement, he was referring to students around the world—including ones in well-regarded Finnish schools. In his book *Finnish Lessons 2.0*, Sahlberg writes that male students in particular are feeling less engaged and less inspired by school, and because of this we ultimately need to change how school is done, including its very function and underlying premises. [4]

Why are students so disengaged, even in the decidedly near-utopian education system of *Finland*? Child poverty is 4x lower in Finland than in the United States,[5] and Finnish teachers are among the most well-educated and highly-respected teachers in the world. The Finns also model their schools around John Dewey's philosophy, which holds "student engagement" as a fundamental concern.

But even in this better place, the teachers still seem to face a systemic problem of students who "lack engagement." They probably do not experience the same level of disengagement as US public school teachers, but it's still there.

Why this is strange is because children are highly engaged with their world. Parents know this, and teachers of younger children know this. As I once observed a pre-K classroom, I remembered all over again how enthusiastic the younglings are in comparison to high school teenagers.

But even that is not so accurate to say, because high school teenagers are much more enthusiastic outside the classroom—as many parents can attest.

I believe it would be more accurate to say that children and teenagers are very active and curious, but on a system level, we do not properly harness their activity and curiosity into "engagement" in school. And we often go further than failing to properly harness their energy; in fact, we systematically transform their potential engagement into boredom, aversion, and pure disinterest.

We take kids who love to learn and turn them into students who supposedly "hate" learning. Does this sound familiar? Maybe it won't to everyone—but it will be familiar to many of us. Carl Sagan has said that "something terrible happens" between Kindergarten and twelfth grade that turns students incurious and unscientific. Albert Einstein said that certain things in school nearly killed his love of science and learning. Mark Twain said that he didn't "let school get in the way of his learning." Many others have echoed this sentiment, even the people—especially the people, it seems—who we look up to as very "smart." Some of the cultural icons we study in school were people who *condemned* school. And in many fundamental ways, school has not changed over the years.

The problem largely lies in how school works. The solution is largely in changing how school works.

Yes, there are out-of-school factors that affect the student psyche, like social, culture, economic, and political factors. But these do not absolve the in-school factors, and like I just said on the previous page, even in societies with less out-of-school issues, there are problems with student engagement in school. When examining schools and classrooms in particular, one explanation for this mass student disengagement is that on a systemic level we do the wrong things to "engage" the students.

It would be wise to turn to a study of motivation. And it doesn't have to be too in-depth, but it has to be deliberately done. Once we have a better understanding of motivation, I believe we will begin to see, and be able to articulate, that many of our policies and practices are *fundamentally de-motivational*. And thus, dis-engaging. Due to school's design in the mainstream, it has always been this way. Perhaps now, for various reasons which include technology, a tumultuous global economy, and modern life, students are more de-motivated by this system than ever before.

Once we acknowledge that many, if not most, of our policies and practices are formed around an incomplete, and highly flawed, concept of motivation—and that our typical strategies to "motivate" often end up doing more harm than good—we can act to change schools so that students will be motivated instead of de-motivated. Then, they will be more engaged. Then, they will learn more and love to learn more. They will be happier and healthier, too. Isn't this what school should be all about?

So if we want students to learn better, and be happier and healthier, we have to understand motivation better. Then, we must deliberately (re-)construct schools and classrooms around the implications of our new understandings.

Schools don't have to be de-motivational or disengaging. If that were true, "school" would simply be a bad idea—a tragic story of children going in motivated, and coming out de-motivated. If schools were simply doomed to undermining peoples' intrinsic motivation, there would be no good reason for them to exist. But this is not a tragic, inevitable story. The school system can evolve. There is a light at the end of the tunnel, and I believe a wider understanding of motivation among educators would bring the teaching profession to a new level. Parents and students who better understand "motivation," as well, can help to push schools, educators, and policies in the right direction.

Vision and Action

The fact that students are so happy to be done with school (or the year, or just the day) in our current system reveals a lot about what school is to the students. They are often not "motivated" by what they are doing—it is frequently the opposite. Students are largely motivated *to get through*, and *be done with*, what they're doing—extrinsic motivation—which is very different than being motivated by whatever you're doing *right now*—intrinsic motivation. This is something the public-relations-people never talk about (they certainly don't understand motivation), with their crazed emphasis on improved scores, grades, and graduation rates—as if these things actually tell us how good of an education the students are getting —or how ethical these students are, or how much they will like to continue learning in the future. Grades, points, scores, awards, and graduation rates don't tell us much about the students, or their education, despite the popular consensus that they do. These superficial indicators simply end up being a smug pat on the back if one "wins the game," or an unnecessary self-loathing if one "fails" or, loses.

But school should not be about winning or losing. The true accomplishment, that so many students miss, is in *learning* itself— loving to do it, finding your place in the world, and improving yourself and the world around you. For school to become a place where students can do this—consistently—we need to rethink schooling. (And not *just* schooling, but yes, schooling).

We can change what we are doing in schools so that no matter the background or personality of the students, our school is ready to work "with" them, rather than simply telling them what they need to do (and then "making" them do it). I found that the education profession—for whatever reasons, including political mandates, social pressures, and the momentum of tradition—has not widely acknowledged, much less put into practice, some critical ideas that have been well-established in science and the humanities. Our practice and policy are *way* behind our theory, but there's no good reason they have to be.

I have done my best to make this book accessible and quickly readable, not just informational. I hope you read my book and find it interesting. But I hope you do more than that. I hope you learn something significant, and then, work together with those around you to change the system. Because it's the *system* that's demotivational—the problem won't be solved without a systemic solution.

Chapter one
Types Of Motivation

Think about a person who goes to their job every day, but hates it. It's unfortunate that this is often the current reality for many workers, and I do not accept it as inevitable, but for now I want to talk about this person's motivation: depending on the circumstances, he may work harder, initially, because it could produce a raise in his salary. Is this employee "motivated?"

Think about a student who turns in an assignment because it "counts." This particular assignment—indeed, many or most of the school assignments—do not matter to this student personally. The student is not necessarily interested in the *content* of the assignment; he doesn't seem to care about math, science, or literature. This student turns in the assignment despite their lack of caring, ...why? Because it was assigned a point value, and therefore, affects his grade.

This grade, we frequently remind the student, can blunt his opportunities, and negatively affect his future.

It can get him in lots of trouble. It can be painful to get a bad grade—or not to get the best grade. Listen, kid: you might have to re-take a class. You might not graduate. You might not get into a good college. Your whole life could be a failure! So, the student turns in the assignment.

Is this student, therefore, *motivated*?

Think about a parent who says to their child: "I will give you an allowance based on your report card grades. Every "A" gets you ten dollars." "B's get you five dollars." "No money for a C."

Anything worse, and you get your privileges taken away. You won't be able to hang out with your friends. You can't do sports. You're not allowed to play video games. No longer will you be able to do whatever it is you really want to do!

Is this parent "motivating" his kid?

Now think of a student who wants to play the violin: she is drawn to the sound and feel of playing. It gives her joy. It is sometimes hard work, but despite this, she practices and practices. She knows this is how she'll get better. This girl seeks out a teacher and more playing experiences on her own.

Is she motivated?

These were trick questions—kind of. It depends on what you mean by "motivation."

Merriam-Webster defines motivation as:

> 1. "The act or process of giving someone a reason for doing something."
>
> 2. "The condition of being eager to act or work."
>
> 3. "A force or influence that causes someone to do something."

Dictionary.com has similar definitions, in summary:

> 1. Providing with reasons to act a certain way.
>
> 2. Having a strong reason to act or accomplish something.
>
> 3. "Inducement" and "incentives."

It seems to me, anyways, that these basic definitions are the extent of our collective understanding of "motivation." And if these definitions summed up motivation, then every person in my given examples would be "motivated," and I would not be writing this book. We could then safely and simply assume that what we're doing in modern schools is "motivating" the students, and this is all that can be done—and we are doomed to an uphill battle forever against naturally de-motivated students.

You know, there's an old proverb that goes like this: "Some knowledge can be worse than no knowledge." I think this often proves to be true in motivation's case.

The dictionary definition, and the conventional understanding, would be "some knowledge," as told in the old proverb.

Many in the social sciences and humanities, however, have explored motivation more deeply than what is suggested by the dictionary definition. And these people have gone beyond what is implied in the conventional wisdom.

Psychologists especially seem obsessed with motivation. The most prominent social scientists to study motivation have been Edward Deci and Richard Ryan, who in the mid-to-late 20th century developed something called "self-determination theory," and built the concepts of "intrinsic" and "extrinsic" motivation.

> "Self-determination theory is a theory of motivation. It is concerned with supporting our natural or intrinsic tendencies to behave in effective and healthy ways." [selfdeterminationtheory.org]

Within *Self-determination Theory* we may find distinct types of motivation, not simply varying "quantities" or "amounts" of motivation. These are,

- "intrinsic" motivation,

   and

- "extrinsic" motivation.

Intrinsic motivation is "motivation that is based on the satisfactions of behaving "for its own sake." [selfdeterminationtheory.org]

Extrinsic motivation refers to "behavior that is driven by external rewards such as money, fame, grades, and praise. This type of motivation arises from outside the individual's sense of self." [verywell.com]

So let's say the people in the beginning of the chapter were not simply "motivated"—we can do better than that.

Is the employee motivated? If the employee's behavior changes based on getting a raise in their paycheck, we can say that this employee has been *extrinsically motivated* to change their behavior.

Is the first student motivated? The student who works on an assignment—only after it is assigned a high-stakes grade—is primarily *extrinsically* motivated to complete that assignment.

Is the second student motivated? The student who works for letter grades because she will get paid for those grades, is primarily *extrinsically* motivated.

Is the violinist motivated? The student who loves playing violin, and is capable of learning and seeking out learning on her own, is primarily *intrinsically* motivated.

I know what some readers might be thinking right now: "We can't have students who are intrinsically motivated to do everything in school." Well, I'll get to that later in the book. For now, it's just important to understand the concept of intrinsic and extrinsic motivation. Bare with me. In the meantime, you might want to re-read this chapter a few times, because it was a quick summary.

—

One core element of Ryan and Deci's "self-determination theory" is a focus on *"how social and cultural factors facilitate or undermine people's sense of volition and initiative."* This idea is highly relevant to educators: various "factors"—some within classrooms and the school environment—can *facilitate* or *undermine* our "volition and initiative."

Various "factors" can either facilitate, or undermine, someone's deeply held motivation. This is the focus of the book you are now reading. **What are those factors—and can we change them?**

Chapter two
As It Relates To Education

How are these different "types" of motivation relevant to education? I would say that few concepts are more relevant. These two distinct types of motivation lead to different attitudes about learning, and different levels of engagement. Whether students are intrinsically or extrinsically motivated will play a major role in determining if the students will *love learning*, and *how well they learn*.

- Certain teaching methods and strategies are "extrinsically" motivating, and put students into completion mode. Not always, but consistently.

- Other teaching methods and strategies are more "intrinsically" motivating, and put students into engagement mode. Not always, but consistently.

Completion mode is how students operate when they are "extrinsically" motivated. It is self-explanatory: students are doing things as if they're simply trying to complete or "get through" that thing, rather than "get into" that thing. This mode of operation, generally speaking, leads to superficial learning. Information is quickly forgotten or is never learned in the first place. Information may be remembered, but often will not be put into a context or wider conceptual framework. It leads to a shallower understanding.

Engagement mode, on the other hand, is how students will tend to operate when they are "intrinsically" motivated. In this mode of operation, students are in a kind of "flow" state. They will experience deeper learning; are more likely to come to a fuller understanding; and will develop better attitudes about learning.

In the following chapters I cite scientific research, done throughout the 20th century and into the 21st century, that supports these claims. Also, it's not difficult to see how it makes sense.

What is going on in students' minds when they are in these different "modes"? Neuroscientists would have their own answer, but I find the biological explanation of "more neural connections," for example, to be insufficient. For an analogy that hits closer to the human experience, consider the following metaphor from a famous educator.

> ## "Reading is not walking on words, it is grasping the soul of them."[6]

Quality reading is not just reciting words and remembering them. That's not all that is happening when we read a good book, or understand a piece of academic writing, or engage with an editorial in the newspaper. More than that, quality reading is developing a conceptual *understanding* of what is being read.

With the metaphor in mind, consider a conversation I've had with students on many occasions (and you can too):

Mr. K: "What is the point of reading if you don't understand what you are reading?"

Student: "The reason to read is getting a grade."

Mr. K: "Is that a good reason for reading?"

[The student nods frantically, as if I asked whether the sky is blue.]

If certain teaching methods and strategies make the students feel "extrinsically" motivated, and extrinsic motivation leads to completion mode, what ultimately happens is that the student is now *walking on words* rather than grasping the soul of them. It's like the words are going "in one ear and out the other."

On the contrary, if a certain teaching method or strategy makes the students feel **intrinsically-motivated**—which leads to "engagement mode"—what happens is that now students are *grasping the soul of* the words. They are making sense of them; truly understanding them.

The importance of this concept for understanding learning and motivation can hardly be overstated. This simple idea is essential for explaining why, as shown through the next several chapters, "intrinsic" motivation is preferable in most situations and especially educational contexts. This is the foundation of authentic motivation in schools.

Extrinsic motivation puts students into **completion mode**, which leads to students *walking on words*.

Intrinsic motivation puts students into **engagement mode,** which leads to students *grasping the soul of them.*

The student who is motivated "extrinsically" will be doing school in "completion" mode. This affects the student's thinking *outside of school* as well. As students grow older and go through school, and are also affected by various home and cultural forces, the students increasingly will be operating *outside* of school in this mindset of completion mode. School learning is not confined to staying within the school walls, just as the school walls do not stop what is learned on the outside. And just because it's not explicitly outlined in the curriculum, doesn't mean it isn't learned.

I'm not just talking about one student or a few. School policies and teaching strategies are often built around the strategy of extrinsic motivation. This in turn leads to students "doing stuff to get it done"—so that they can receive rewards and awards—and so that they can avoid punishments and so-called "consequences. "

Consequently, these students are walking on words, or numbers or ideas, rather than grasping the soul of them.

Alfie Kohn has drawn the analogy that "we give students a brick and another brick and another brick and another brick and another brick until we think the students have a house. But most of what they end up having is *a pile of bricks*—and not for very long."[7] This is the direct result of an extrinsic approach to school. This is perhaps the main problem with the school system, and the more you look for this problem, the more obvious it becomes. Honest and reflective educators and parents should be able to tell the metaphor is accurate.

(In later chapters, I illustrate some ways to specifically tell the difference between an "intrinsically" and "extrinsically" motivated student, or set of students.)

The path of collecting as many irrelevant "bricks" as possible, then to showcase how many bricks you collected, is why school is often perceived by the students as frustrating, pointless, or simply a waste of time. Because, in large part, it is. What else do you call so much information that is never used, or even learned in the first place? Schools and educators are "motivating" the students *extrinsically*, and then the students begin to walk on words rather than grasp the soul of them. It is hardly a choice for the students, who must pass through the system in order to "succeed."

The pile of "bricks," or disconnected bits of information that the students obtain, become largely useless over time. Eventually, most of them tumble over, and vanish. Most of what we "learned" in school is forgotten, without purpose, or just a bunch of information rather than actual *understanding*.

Just as unfortunate is that students become less likely to build a "house" in the future—because they have come to believe that "learning" is about collecting the bricks of information that were presented by authorities. Students lose interest in "learning"—very much because we "motivated" them in the wrong way.

—

Here are some words that align with the idea of intrinsic motivation, which leads to "engagement mode," which leads to *grasping the soul of* words, numbers, and ideas.

- Joy
- Curiosity
- Interest
- Passion
- Intrigue
- Inspiration
- Purpose
- Autonomy
- Appropriateness
- Self-initiated

If we want to motivate students "intrinsically," the best thing we can do is create a good environment for learning and then "inspire" and guide them along, while they explore ideas. For intrinsic motivation's sake, it would be best to start with the students' interests, and work outward from there. (Public schools currently operate in the opposite direction, with external goals or standards as the starting point, and then the teacher trying desperately to somehow connect the external goals to all of the different students' interests.)

Though it can be difficult to do in practice—and it is not how the schools system operates (in general)—the "intrinsic" strategy is simple in essence. The second and third sections of this book are about putting the concept into practice.

Here are some words that align with "extrinsic motivation," which leads to completion mode—resulting in superficial learning, short memory retention, and knowledge without a context or practical purpose.

- Comply
- Control
- Forced
- Bribed
- Mandate
- Boring
- Uninteresting
- Deadline (mixed)
- Doing something for the reward
- Doing something so you won't get a consequence or punishment
- *Because I said so*

We could even think of each group of words as a "family" under intrinsic or extrinsic motivation.

There are a few good ways I have discovered for conceptualizing these approaches, or strategies, to "motivating" people. For extrinsic motivation, one concept is *punishments and rewards*, which Alfie Kohn calls "two sides of the same coin." Another illustration of the extrinsic approach is "carrots and sticks," which essentially means the same as punishments and rewards.

Carrots = *Rewards / Awards / Conditional Praise*
Sticks = *Threats / Punishments / Consequences*

(Two sides of the extrinsic coin.)

The extrinsic approach can be good for getting *temporary* compliance, sometimes. But overall, in an attempt to solve the problem of "unmotivated" students, the extrinsic approach ends up causing a more significant problem. It makes the problem *worse*—by entrenching, and contributing to, a lack of caring about whatever is supposed to be the learner's focus (mathematics, for example). The "extrinsic" approach to motivating people—in the deeper analysis, and in the long-term—is actually *de-motivational*. It disengages students from understanding—and from *wanting* to understand.

Educators and parents may *wish* to motivate students intrinsically, but what our school system broadly does not understand is that the *extrinsic approach,* which includes an infinite toolbox of "inducements" and "incentives," **undermines** intrinsic motivation, thus sapping away the students' potential, harming their attitudes and ethical development, and even causing physical and psychological illness.

In order for students to become intrinsically-motivated, like they were as young children—and like adults are in certain situations—the first step is to gradually diminish, and ultimately **abandon,** extrinsic motivation as an educational strategy.

—

"Extrinsic motivation" is essentially the strategy of choice for our school system because we feel that we must constantly get students to do things that initially they do not want to do, for whatever reason. One major strategy in moving away from the extrinsic approach would be to make the school system more along the lines of what students "want" to learn in the first place. This is not the entire solution, and it can be complicated, but it is one part of the solution.

Some critics and cynics surely would counter this suggestion with the conventional wisdom that "we can't always do what we want in school." But to that argument I have two replies, and the first is "why not?"

That was me being only somewhat hyperbolic. While I understand that perhaps students cannot *always* do what they want—and the younger they are, the more this may be true—students can certainly do what they want *much more often than they are currently doing in school.*

We have a cultural idea that "doing what we want" will be less educationally-effective, precisely because it's desirable, and that we should feel guilty anytime we don't feel stressed in school. Logically this does not follow, and from an educational psychology perspective it's just plain wrong. Why would we believe that studying our interests will lead to worse learning? And why do we often believe that students are not capable of being interested in "intellectual" stuff? If they're not interested in learning, that is not a stone cold fact of their nature but a clue as to how they've been nurtured, and an indication of whether or not we are creating an intellectual environment for them.

My second response is that even if students cannot always do "whatever they want," there are ways to respectfully give them more autonomy within a limited curriculum and rule set, and make a "boring" thing better—or an initially "uninteresting" thing, more interesting. This is what good teachers try to do, typically. But in my view, we don't even do *this* enough. We often assume the students must simply bend to us, or simply "learn to like it," and if they don't, it's their fault.

To look at a specific example: if high school students over-whelmingly don't want to take "algebra," then (after we seriously deliberate on whether algebra is in fact necessary for every student in high school), we'd change how we teach math in the classroom to make alegebra more practical, more interesting, and maybe even more fun. In other words, we commit to becoming better educators, and to treating students more intelligently and more humanely, rather than relying on compulsion and gimmicky "incentives" to do the motivation for us.

There are a lot of things we can do differently to make algebra (or whatever) more intrinsically-valuable, which would lead to students operating more consistently in "engagement mode," and thus, learning better and enjoying learning more. This would not just be a matter of making teaching more "entertaining"—it would involve changes in the way we teach, what our priorities are, and what we expect from students. Generally it should include the removal of extrinsic inducements and incentives, which sabotage the students' intrinsic motivation.

Chapter three

The Power Of Intrinsic Motivation,
The Lost Potential Of Extrinsic Motivation

"Behind every achievement exists the motivation which is at the foundation of it." [8]

-Albert Einstein

Behind every achievement is *motivation*. That is a significant statement, from a significant thinker, and illustrates the incredible importance of motivation. Think about what it means. Without Einstein's motivation, he wouldn't have become Einstein, and his incredible accomplishments which defined modern science may not have happened. He would not have reached his potential. We as a society would have lost so much.

Now imagine that actually happening for most people who go through the school system, to become *de-motivated*. It is unimaginable how much we lose when this happens. And it surely does.

In a speech that Albert Einstein once gave to an education audience, from which I drew the opening quote, Einstein describes a few different ways of motivating the student:

- "fear and compulsion" [*extrinsic motivation*]
- "ambitious desire for authority and distinction" [*extrinsic*

- *motivation*] and
- "loving interest in the object and a desire for truth and understanding" [*intrinsic motivation*].

Albert Einstein elaborated on the importance of nurturing intrinsic motivation, which exists in everyone:

> *"...to divine curiosity which every healthy child possesses."*

He described how intrinsic motivation is systematically diminished through childhood:

> *"...but which so often is weakened early."*

Which kind of motivation does Albert Einstein believe is preferable? In his address, he continued:

> "To me the worst thing seems to be for a school principally to work with methods of fear, force, and artificial authority. Such treatment destroys the sound sentiments, the sincerity, and the self-confidence of the pupil. It produces the submissive subject."

Well, Einstein didn't have a high opinion of "fear" and "authority," which are extrinsic "motivators"—external reasons for us think or act. What, then, was his solution?

> "It is not so hard to keep the school free from the worst of all evils. Give into the power of the teacher the fewest possible coercive measures"

...so that:

"the only source of the pupil's respect for the teacher is the human and intellectual qualities of the latter."

In other words, teachers should teach through intellectual passion and their own joys, which the students would come to admire.

It is important *not* to teach through force and discipline—which would turn the students away from learning, and the subject being studied. Mr. Smartypants goes on:

"The most important motive for work in the school and life is pleasure in work, pleasure in its results, and the knowledge of the value of the result to the community."

(This is essentially a description of **intrinsic motivation.**)

Einstein also says in his address that awakening a love of learning is "the greatest task of the school." Not just one task of the school, or a great task of the school. **The greatest** task of the school.

Albert Einstein's pontification on the purpose of education, and the methods of educators, match countless mission statements of modern schools and the education philosophies of teachers. Why, then, must we deliberate on this concept? We must do so because words and actions are not the same. The problem in our day, as well as Albert Einstein's, it seems, is that we are not doing the right things to match our well-intended goals.

Our words and wishes do not match our actions. We want intrinsic motivation from the students, but we are not doing the right things to nurture it. We are destroying it by accident, often not even realizing it.

I have gone through several of Albert Einstein's speeches and essays. He advocates consistently for nurturing curiosity, rather than compelling people to learn, and has said that he is "*nothing special, only passionately curious.*"

Albert Einstein also wrote that there were teachers and teaching methods which turned him away from his favorite subject (science, duh) by using methods of coercion.

Thankfully, it was temporary, but it is not temporary for everyone. Some are turned away forever.

—

I would say there are three broad categories under *the purpose of education*.

1. The disposition to learn. We could call this "love of learning," "continuing to learn in the future," "learning how and why to learn," and so on. John Dewey said "the purpose of education is more education"; teachers and school mission statements often say that their job is to create "life-long learners." Socrates said that education is not the filling of a pail, but the lighting of a fire. Everyone who is serious about education thinks this is very important, maybe even the most important goal of education.

2. General well-being. Education is about improving our lives as a whole—individually and collectively. This includes many aspects that are not necessarily academic or intellectual, like the physical, emotional, social, psychological, and ethical aspects. We want to live good, joyful, happy lives. That typically doesn't just happen on its own—it improves our odds, at least, if we could explicitly learn how to do this. Through education we learn about making choices, we learn about the human condition, we learn about diet and nutrition, we learn philosophy and ethics, we learn vocational skills, and we learn to be able to help ourselves in general. We learn social skills, we learn about our society, and we learn how and why to affect the world around us. That is what education could be, at least, and perhaps what it should be, whenever it isn't.

If education is not a tool for personal and societal well-being, then I think it's not much of an education at all.

3. Excellence. Education is about learning to be "better" at specific things. This includes skill-based and knowledge-based pursuits. All pursuits include some combination of skills and knowledge, but some pursuits (for example, college professors) are more heavily knowledge-based, while others (for example, olympic athletes) are more skills-based. Education is a tool to take us further, and make us better, in any field—including, but not limited to, the academic domain. We learn knowledge and skills, not just to be healthy and well, but *to know* and be better at stuff.

Critical thinking and creative thinking could fall into this category, since these are about learning to be "better" thinkers.

Purposes of education #1: **the disposition to learn** and #2: **well being** would be the "heart" in Aristotle's sage wisdom, *"education without the heart is no education at all."* And for these first two categories it is clear that motivating students "intrinsically" is a better approach. Any comparison to extrinsic motivation would end almost before it began, because intrinsically-motivated people fare so much better when we're looking at positive learning dispositions, and greater health and well-being.

We become better and more curious learners, and are more physically and psychologically healthy, when we are "intrinsically" motivated. (In a moment, and through the next few chapters, I will review studies and give reasoning to support this.)

For the third category, excellence—which is the main focus of this chapter—it is tempting in our culture to believe that "extrinsic" motivation is required. The idea goes that we have to "make" people do things in order for them to learn or accomplish those things. And we do believe this in some capacity. If we didn't, why would we so often teach and parent this way?

But this line of thinking is simply not an accurate assessment of learning and human life. People who are primarily "intrinsically" motivated *do* become excellent, at least as well as, but probably much more often than, people who are/were "extrinsically" motivated.

That's why this chapter is called *the power of intrinsic motivation:* it is the best way for humans to reach their potential. And the chapter has a dual title, *the lost potential of extrinsic motivation,* because the power of each generation is left locked away when we teach our students to shut down their intrinsic motivation, and go through school and life collecting rewards and avoiding punishments. We as a society are far less than we could be for having been motivated extrinsically.

Extrinsic Motivation: An Illustration

In the movie *Men in Black,* Agent "K" introduces Agent "J" to a technological device that erases the memory of whoever is on the receiving end. It looks like a cigar case, operates like a camera flash—and if you're looking in the direction of the device when it activates, you're not going to remember what you just saw or did.

Thus goes the "meme" with the *Men in Black* pointing the memory-erasure device at us:

Finished studying? *Good.*

Then comes the flash of light, and we forget. For a student, the "flash of light" is *the test.* Maybe it's the end of the course. Or, when a little more lucky, it's a year or two.

The human mind may have its limits. But this simple meme is

also an indictment of our school system. "School things" seem to be lost so much more quickly, and more often, than things which are learned in a better context and for a greater purpose.

Everyone knows the phenomenon: You studied for the test. You studied because the teacher gave you the criteria on which you'd be "graded." You didn't necessarily study at your own discretion. You didn't necessarily study because you had an interest in whatever you're studying. And after you get your grade, you forget, if you can.

Or maybe you forget even if you don't want to forget—even if you wanted to remember—because you walked on words instead of grasping the soul of them. The problem is that you weren't fully engaged in learning, because you weren't intrinsically-motivated.

And what if that information from your class did make it further into your life? Well, it might be the exception. And even if you do remember, you'd have to ask if that material was worth remembering.

How useful is it? How deeply do you understand that thing? Are you even sure that one thing you remember from that one class is *true*...?

Not everything we once learned in school is gone, and not all of our time spent in school was worthless. Of course! If school was *all* a waste of time, far fewer people would advocate for it, including myself. I am not saying that school is pointless, even in its current form that I find lacking. Some things are learned in school, and some of those things that we retain are worth learning.

What I'm saying is that we spend ten to twenty thousand hours in school, and we don't have anything close to that to show for it. I'm saying that we can do much better, and by learning about the concept of motivation, supported by science research and a better depth of reasoning, we can transform the system and harness the power of what education could really be.

—

"In the middle of the last century, two young scientists conducted experiments that should have changed the world—but did not."[9]

-Daniel Pink, *Drive*

STUDIES

In 1949, a professor of psychology named Harry Harlow, along with a few colleagues, conducted a simple experiment with primates. Well, it would have been a simple procedural test for a human—but not for a monkey, who would require specific, deliberate training to be successful. Or so they thought.

The monkeys were given puzzles that required three steps to solve: pulling out a pin, undoing a hook, and lifting a hinged cover. What the researchers found, unexpectedly, is that the monkeys solved these puzzles without being taught how to solve them. The monkeys did not have to be "reinforced" for the "correct" behaviors in order to solve them. They were neither instructed nor incentivized to solve the puzzles. They simply did.

The results of this experiment did not fit into any explanation of the behavioral scientists at the time.

The next part of the experiment was even more unexpected. Though the researchers could reluctantly form an explanation for what had just occurred—that there was an "intrinsic" desire on the part of the primates to complete the puzzle—they still figured, *obviously*, that rewarding the monkeys with yummy food would increase their proficiency in solving the puzzle.

But, contrary to the conventional wisdom, or scientific understanding of the time, when the monkeys were given tangible, edible rewards, they made *more* errors and solved the puzzles *less often* than when no reward was given.

This was the beginning of a string of psychology experiments in the mid-to-late 20th century which would show essentially the same effect in humans. These experiments on motivation and performance would be conducted through a variety of cultures, situations, age groups, and with various types of rewards, pointing strongly to the same conclusion: Rewards contingent on performance undermine that performance, and interest in the task itself.

One famous study in the field was "the candle problem." In 1962, a graduate student named Sam Glucksberg performed an experiment in which undergraduate students were told to solve a problem: they are given a box of matches, a box of thumbtacks, and a candle—and then were told to attach the candle to the wall—without having wax drip on the table in the process.

The solution requires some out-of-the-box thinking. To solve the problem, it was necessary to utilize the box itself (that initially held the thumbtacks) as a platform for the candle. The solution is not apparent due to the way the materials are set up—it appears initially that the box is only a *container* for the materials, and not an actual material to use in solving the problem.

What happened in the experiment is that students took much longer to solve the problem when they were told beforehand that they'd be paid for solving the problem quickly. The results suggested that people who are offered a reward for solving a problem are *less able* to think quickly and/or creatively.

Around the same time, a long-term study was being conducted on undergraduate students at the Art Institute in Chicago. Students were surveyed on their attitudes toward work, and questions were asked to determine whether the students were more "intrinsically" or "extrinsically" motivated during their studies. What researchers found is that the students who were more "intrinsically" and less "extrinsically" motivated during school, were typically more successful later in life—at their craft and in their professional career.

More experiments in the 1970s would confirm that rewards diminish task performance. For a more thorough reading of this research, I recommend the books *Punished by Rewards* and *Drive*, but I will summarize a few of the studies that were included:

- Children who were told they would receive candy for getting more answers correct, ended up getting less answers correct.[10]
- Elementary students who were promised candy or prizes—even candy and prizes they specifically indicated they enjoyed—performed worse on the researcher's given tasks.[11]
- High school students were given various tasks that tested their memory and creativity; the students who were rewarded did not perform as well, no matter the task, as the students who were not rewarded.[12]
- College students frequently fared worse on recognition tests and problem solving when they were offered monetary rewards.[13]

Many more studies, by different researchers, with different experiments, and conducted with different age groups and in different settings, and published in different journals—would begin to reach the conclusion that external incentives diminish task performance.

> "By the 1980s, anyone who kept up with this sort of research would have found it impossible to claim that the best way to get people to perform well is to dangle a reward in front of them."[14]

> -Alfie Kohn

Kohn also quotes a prominent 20th century social psychologist, Kenneth McGraw, who reached a conclusion based on this research through the mid-1970s:

> "Incentives will have a detrimental effect on performance when two conditions are met: first, when the task is interesting enough for subjects that the offer of incentives is a superfluous source of motivation; second, when the solution to the task is open-ended enough that the steps leading to a solution are not immediately obvious."[15] (Kohn quotes McGraw)

This is a telling conclusion, and summarizes the point that an extrinsic approach to motivation harms sophisticated thinking, deeper learning, and long-term development of ability. Incentives are also unnecessary when the tasks are interesting to the learners. (So it is educators' job to continue making the effort to offer a relevant curriculum, and interesting tasks—letting students choose much of what and how to study in the process. I discuss this more specifically in later chapters.)

How would we accomplish "making tasks interesting to the learners"? There are many ways, but the major point I'm trying to make right now is that the first step is to remove the extrinsic motivators. That is the *first step*, not the end goal or entire solution.

The science is clear in this domain, and the research on rewards and task performance has only become more solid over the years. Kohn's book was published in 1993 and updated in 1999. Dan Pink's "Drive" was published in 2011. Both confidently concluded that extrinsic motivators diminish task performance while undermining intrinsic motivation. There are certain occasions when this conclusion is not true—or when it is less true—but it is true much more often than it is false. It is a solid general guideline for rethinking teacher practices, and building a new foundation to our education system.

—

Consider our personal heroes and cultural legends—all the geniuses, inventors, scientists, writers, and timeless artists. Do you think they were primarily motivated "intrinsically" or "extrinsically"?

Ponder, sure, but it's an easy question to answer. The greatest musicians were primarily motivated by music itself. The greatest scientists were motivated by the nature of nature; of how human beings exist socially and in nature. The greatest writers have generally loved writing itself—more than anything else.

Now, if the greatest people were primarily "intrinsically" motivated, what does that tell us about the "wisdom" of an overall extrinsic approach to "motivating" students? Especially considering that extrinsic motivation strongly tends to undermine intrinsic motivation? (This is explored more in the next chapter.)

At best, students will simply not be learning at their full potential, which is a shame.

I have found that there are intelligent people out there who acknowledge scientific studies, but also have a feeling that the studies are distant and impersonal (understandable), and so they are still difficult to fully believe—especially if the scientific "theory" seems to contradict personal experience. (For example: when teachers believe that grades and consequences "work," and therefore we can/should use them.)

And it's good to be skeptical, even of scientific research, because some research is not very good or is simply incomplete. It's difficult to read about research that seems to contradict our own judgment and personal experience.

For those who are not fully convinced by the body of research summarized here, or maybe do not trust me completely, fine. Let's discover patterns and draw conclusions from our own experiences. We should continue to think about this logically and rationally. We should make sure that these ideas really are "practical." We should continue to make our own observations.

"There is no question that in virtually all circumstances in which people are doing things in order to get rewards, extrinsic tangible rewards undermine intrinsic motivation."[16] -Albert Einstein

What the heck? Albert Einstein is the most famous scientist of all, and here's why I just quoted Einstein after saying that we should not simply rely on science research. The quoted observation was not a result of scientific research because that was not the focus of his research. It was made before 20th century social scientists did their research on motivation and task performance; before Deci and Ryan thoroughly illustrated that extrinsic motivation undermines intrinsic motivation; and before the theory of self-determination came into being.

Albert Einstein may have been a scientist, but his field of study was not psychology. His formal focus was not even within the social sciences. Einstein was a theoretical physicist—what they call a "natural" scientist—someone who studies "universal" as opposed to human and social phenomena.

As a great scientist and mathematician, Albert Einstein was not simply confined to observing space and time and physical matter. He was a great *observer*. As a leading thinker of the human race, Einstein was aptly concerned with human problems, questions, and solutions. He used his understanding of nature, and general observations of society, to comment on social life and the human condition.

As I showed earlier, Einstein frequently commented on education and human behavior. Even though he did not formally study "motivation," he had much to say on it. Albert Einstein did not come to these conclusions about motivation in a lab, or by looking at the stars. He carefully and critically watched the human world go by.

What if I suggested that we can make the same observations he did?—not necessarily by putting on lab coats, reading peer-reviewed studies, or solving abstract equations—but by being *scientific-minded*. You can be a scientific thinker without being a professional scientist.

"Honesty is the first chapter in the book of wisdom"
-Socrates

What helps in being honest and seeing the truth is to have a framework through which to view a problem, such as:

1. There are two different "kinds" of motivation: intrinsic and extrinsic.
2. Extrinsic motivation leads to worse task performance and recall of information than intrinsic motivation.

Now we can look at the world—what is going on around us, in the classroom, for example—and see if this is true. Or, as a scientist would say: we'd check if the observations and real-world evidence match our hypothesis.

A simple question for teachers to ask themselves, for example, is whether students retain information better when they are learning for a test *versus* when they have chosen and thoroughly enjoy a particular topic of study.

Then, teachers can do their own experiment. Anyone can ask

questions to the students—individually, or as a group—about the assignment they did last week *for a grade,* that they were "enticed" to do but did not actually feel interested in doing.

Find out what those students remember, and what they truly understand—especially with reference to what was "covered" in class and what was "intended" for them to learn.

Ask the students a month later about what was was on their test. Find out at the end of the course—not through a paper test, but a dialogue with the student—how much the student really understands about what was taught and what was intended.

Do this informally, as part of a conversation, precisely because the students would be able to prepare for a final exam. Everything changes when you get them with a spontaneous question or conversation. Through a simple dialogue, we can often get a better idea of what a student truly remembers and understands.

I did this all the time as a substitute teacher. One technique I used frequently was to take a student's paper off their desk (nicely, while smiling and joking), and then asking the student about the stuff that is on the page I just watched them complete.

It was rare for most of them to be able to explain anything on that page they were just doing. I could show over and over again that "completing" something is not the same as "understanding" something.

It is obvious, and I can show anyone the results if they would like a demonstration.

When students *could* repeat and remember what they answered, they rarely had an understanding of the significance of that thing; or the proper context that made that thing important or unimportant, relevant or irrelevant, true or untrue.

Students are constantly "doing" things, but not understanding or even remembering those things.

We reap what we sow, and this is the fruit of the extrinsic seed.

Students are doing lots and lots of stuff and don't even know what the hell they are doing, what they're learning, or why. Then, they forget most of it anyways.

—

Instead, teachers can engage students in conversations and projects that they seem to enjoy. Let them choose topics, or sub-topics, in which they are interested. Then, we can find out what the students remember at the end of the class; the end of the day; the end of the month, or the end of the year. Or next year. And not just what they remember. What they understand.

I bet that teachers and parents who perform this "experiment" would end up agreeing with social psychologists, Albert Einstein's observations, and my point of view in this book that extrinsic motivation not only undermines the student's enjoyment of the task or topic, but also, the ability for students to remember at length, understand in depth, and do very well in the end.

Chapter four

The Dangers Of An Extrinsic Approach

"If we only do things out of fear of punishment, or promise of reward, we are a sorry lot indeed."

—*Albert Einstein*

Is it necessary to waste all this time and generate all this grief in order to "learn"? So that students can *get a job one day?* Especially if there's a better way?

And if there's more reason—of even greater significance—to move away from an extrinsic approach?

If only an extrinsic approach were simply "less effective" for making people smarter and better. Maybe then it wouldn't be so terrible, and maybe then I wouldn't feel the need to write a book about it. But the problem with being extrinsically motivated runs deeper than worse task performance, or a little lost interest. It is not just lost potential or a waste of time. It is much worse than a waste of time. It is very harmful. It is a disease. And far more than kids on a skateboard could ever be, an education system that relies on extrinsic motivation is a menace to society.

In 1969, two decades after Harlow's first experiment, a psychology student named Edward Deci designed an experiment in which human subjects would be asked to reproduce a sophisticated game puzzle. Some of the subjects were offered a monetary reward, and others were not. The experiment was complex and took place over the course of three days.

Deci wanted to discover whether (and how much) the human subjects continued to play with the puzzle once he left the room. Deci sneakily told the subjects that he had to do experiment-related tasks in an adjacent room, and there would be some down time. But actually, through a one-way window he would continue to evaluate the subjects after he left.

What he found on the third day of the experiment is that the people who were rewarded with money spent significantly less time playing with the puzzles than the ones who were not given the monetary reward.

Consider another study, a paper published in the *Journal of Research in Education* titled "The effect of mandatory reading logs on children's motivation to read."[17] In this study, the researcher Sarah S. Pak of Princeton University examined the effects of mandatory reading logs on students' interest in "recreational" reading. One group of elementary students were given the *option* to keep "reading logs"—they could do them, or not do them—and the other group was compelled to do the reading logs: they *had* to do them.

You can read the entire study yourself if you want, which is referenced in the endnotes, but the researcher ultimately concluded what so many others in the field had already concluded: extrinsic inducements produced a drop in intrinsic motivation. Making the students "log" their reading—as we so frequently do, as a "normal" part of being a teacher—*made them not like to read.*

> "Students with mandatory logs expressed declines in both interest and attitudes towards recreational reading in comparison to peers with voluntary logs, and attitudes towards academic reading decreased signifi-

cantly from pre to post test across conditions."

Then Sarah S. Pak suggested: "Future research should explore alternate ways to promote reading."

This is a hint of what is so terrible about extrinsic motivators. It takes the joy out of our lives, and ultimately is de-motivating in that it stops us from wanting to do things that maybe we would have done otherwise. But that is not all.

It makes us unhealthy

On the website selfdeterminationtheory.org, we could quickly find the following summary, concluded from decades of thorough research, about extrinsic versus intrinsic goals:

> *"Extrinsic goals such as financial success, appearance, and popularity/fame have been specifically contrasted with intrinsic goals such as community, close relationships, and personal growth, with the former [extrinsic goals] more likely associated with lower wellness and greater ill-being."*

Lower wellness and greater ill-being is partially a reference to our physical health, but it also makes us...

Psychologically unwell

"Using extrinsic incentives… often contributes to feelings of anxiety and even helplessness," writes Kohn in *Punished by Rewards*. "…some children, instead of rebelling against coercion, simply relinquish their autonomy." [18]

Giving up one's own sense of control does not simply go away when students leave the classroom. Extrinsic inducements, especially when so frequently used, are like a psychological whip. Even when the initial wounds go away, the scars remain, and the whipping has changed us permanently. We will be fearful of the whip in the future, and hardly will make an attempt to escape its invisible threat.

Self-determination theory is concerned with "the willingness to continue doing," and one of the most clear findings in this subset of psychology is that extrinsic motivators undermine the willingness to continue doing, even in contexts that are different from the original situation.

> "Controlling environments have been shown consistently to reduce people's interest in whatever they are doing, even when they are doing things that would be highly motivating in other contexts."[19] (Kohn)

Kohn cites studies in which students in controlling classrooms displayed lower self-esteem and intrinsic motivation than those in classrooms of more "supportive" teachers.[20] From another study, he summarizes that "a highly-controlling approach used with one task reduced people's interest in a second, entirely different task."[21]

Tool of control

It brings us to the major purpose of extrinsic motivators. Though they are supposed to be a strategy for inducing learning, that is something they are actually quite bad at doing. The truth is that extrinsic motivators are first and foremost about *control*. If you don't believe me on that, imagine the situations in which extrinsic motivators are used. They are typically used by the more powerful party to get what it wants from the less powerful. Do you think that is a coincidence?

Now, we can debate to what ends the controls are being used. A teacher may say, "oh, I was getting the student to comply because I wanted them to learn." And that very well may be the intention, and in certain situations, it can be true. After all, if you have a student who won't go to class unless "made" to—or a class-room full of students who won't sit down and shut up, and "don't want to learn"—it appears to educators that we will simply need to find a quick way to make the students comply in order to "get their education." Thus, we turn to extrinsic motivators, which can be decent tools for getting quick compliance.

But the costs are too high. This is a dangerous road to go down, and clearly, the strategy has a very limited effect on what the rebellious students (who we are trying to coerce) truly learn in the end. The insistence that this path is necessary—blocks out the paving of a better one—and this route we have taken yields major consequences to our individual and collective psyche. This is a strategy that has led to authoritarian environments in schools and classrooms. Manipulating the students through extrinsic induce-ments and incentives; punishments and rewards; carrots and sticks; reductions in autonomy; and so on, are *a part of the education they are receiving.* The students learn a lot of the wrong things about learning: for example, that the topic is inherently uninteresting and one must be "made" to learn it. And ultimately, students learn the lesson of power imbalance. Authority is simply to be obeyed. If you do not obey, the more powerful person has a right to bully you into compliance.

> "The average American high school is excellent preparation for the real world, if you live in a totali-tarian society."[22]
> —Alfie Kohn

Totalitarian is a strong word, and yet the argument is difficult to counter. Students are extremely controlled in schools, and if this is preparation for "the real world," logically it must be preparation for an extremely controlled world.

In some ways, we live in an authoritarian society, and school is simply echoing those tendencies. The political realm and the workplace can seem seem this way at times—with the powerful bringing their ultimate authority down on those who are simply employees or regular citizens.

In other ways, school is its own monster. Even in the workplace, at least in many areas, workers are typically not so controlled as students are in schools. Most adults would not tolerate the kind of manipulation that students must tolerate in school. And to some extent, jobs are chosen, which softens the iron grip. School, on the other hand, is compulsory.

Again, we can debate the ends of control, but we cannot deny that students *are* highly controlled in school—and that this highly controlling environment contributes to poor health and bad attitudes about learning.

I can easily write more on this, but I feel that I've gotten dark enough already, and I don't think further explanation is necessary. The danger of extrinsic motivation lies in its diminishing of our human potential, but more than that, a strategy of extrinsic motivation justifies the powerful to do anything in the name of simply "motivating" someone else. Many of the things that the powerful end up doing are ultimately not justified. But by employing the psychological warfare of extrinsic motivation, the powerful can hold their grip on the powerless. Anyone concerned with basic issues of justice and ethics must grapple with this dilemma. Extrinsic motivators are a terribly destructive way to motivate. Is it worth it? Is there another way?

—

"Extrinsic motivators are most dangerous when offered for something we want children *to want* to do."[23]

—Alfie Kohn

We must be concerned with "how" we are teaching students to think and do, not just "what" we *intend* for them to learn. Educators want their students to love learning, and to continue learning in the future—so we should do what is more likely to make that happen.

I find Kohn's guideline to be excellent. Extrinsic motivators are most dangerous for the things we want students *to want* to do. Want them to love learning? Then, why would we attempt to motivate them "extrinsically" to learn? That would not make sense.

Do we want students to *want* to be healthy? To be intelligent? To be wise, ethical, and good friends?

Then why motivate them "extrinsically"? The research is in, and it's *been* in. At best, extrinsic motivators are no better. Often worse, they are consistently counterproductive. At their worst, they are destructive to the kind of people and sort of society that we want.

In the face of all this evidence and reason, there is only one answer to why we would continue to use extrinsic motivators as an educational strategy—and it's not a great reason, but at least I can understand it: *"Because it's easier that way."* And it's simply hard to change.

Well, that is our challenge then. If we educators see ourselves as a beneficent force, we must strive to do things the better way, even if it's initially more difficult. We must make the effort to change ourselves, to persuade others, and work together. Of course, it's not just educators' responsibility, but we do have *some* responsibility to make a change, even if others are not going to help us. (But we should urge non-educators to take responsibility, too.)

It's made easier when we keep the truth in mind, and the end goal, which is a world full of curious, healthy, and self-initiating life-long learners. That would be a much more wise, intelligent, and beautiful world than this one.

Such a world would look very different than ours. I have no doubt that it would be a much better one. How will you contribute to making it possible?

Part II
Confronting the "extrinsic" approach

Chapter Five
Extrinsic Everywhere

"Worse, these practices have infiltrated our schools, where we ply our future workforce with iPods, cash, and pizza coupons to "incentivize" them to learn. Something has gone wrong." [24]

-Dan Pink

Once the difference between intrinsic and extrinsic motivation is understood; once the problems with extrinsic motivation (and the power of intrinsic motivation) are understood; and once it's understood that extrinsic motivation erodes intrinsic motivation—it's time to go look around the schools.

Let's look at what's on the walls in the hallway and the classrooms. Let's listen to what the adults in school are saying when they speak to the students. Let's solicit the students' opinions—and take note of their responses to certain assignments and requests.

It's time to examine our discipline policies, and our teaching/learning policies, and ask: will this nurture the students' extrinsic "motivation," or their intrinsic motivation?

Anyone who really wants to know what's going on should do this. I've done it myself, for several years, and tried to prove myself (and Alfie Kohn) wrong. Here is a lot of what you'll find in the schools, and most wouldn't be surprised when I say this: you'll find lots of punishments and rewards, carrots and sticks, threats and bribes.

You'll find what I said in the preface of this book, which is adults asking and begging students to be intrinsically motivated, while simultaneously training them to be extrinsically motivated.

Points, grades, praise, ratings, ranks, popcorn, candy, cookies, parties, field trips, scholarships, honors, acceptance, pats on the back. Extrinsic everywhere. It's the main force of "motivation." Intrinsic motivation ("the joy of knowing and doing") is the exception, not the rule. Attempts at intrinsic motivation are not entirely absent—but they are strongly and persistently overshadowed by attempts to motivate "extrinsically."

Sure, some of the things I mentioned aren't "bad," per se— there's nothing inherently wrong with popcorn, field trips, personal compliments, or gift cards. What's bad is in *how* they are used: contingently. We ask and demand the students to learn *so that* they can earn these rewards; *so that* they can avoid the consequences.

As Kohn says in *Punished by Rewards*, it's the strategy of "do this and you'll get that." Daniel Pink in *Drive* calls them "if-then" rewards. Whatever you want to call it, it's the brick and mortar of our school system's approach to motivation.

Punishment is problematic in its own right, but *contingent rewards* are the silent destroyer that pervade our schools. Punishment is slowly being phased out in schools, but rewards are as strong as ever—or stronger than ever—because it is assumed they are better and more humane than punishment. Well, they are slightly more humane, but not really by much (read Kohn's book, or just the title of his book).

The schools *fundamentally rely* on rewards for their power to "motivate" extrinsically. And the worst extrinsic motivator of all is the one that is most personal, most used, and therefore the most negatively influential.

Grades (poison)

Imagine that everyone is constantly pushing a nutritional product in your face: It's the best thing you could do for your health and your future. You need more and more of it, and you need to do it better and better—all the time.

But actually, it's not nutritious. It's poison. Welcome to grade hell.

Grades have been effectively debunked as a practice for decades, first through argument, and then through educational psychology. And yet grades are still universally and overwhelmingly accepted as good and necessary in our school system. Questioning their basis in the first place is almost unheard of—it's on the level of questioning a high priest if God is Really Real. (Actually, said high priest may be better at entertaining heresy than most people are at considering the non-sanctity of grades.)

There are many substantial arguments against the practice of grades, which I will explore in my next book—but when it comes to motivation, they are the most salient extrinsic motivators and the ones that are most often used. And guess what?

> *"When people use rewards to motivate, that's when they're most demotivating."*[25]

> -Dan Pink

In the long term, and in the deeper analysis, grades are *extremely* de-motivational. More than anything else we do in schools, grades teach students that learning itself is not its own reward. "Learning" is not an end in itself, it is a means to an end: a means to getting the grade. This outlook turns students into a bunch of "task completers."

A former student of mine, when asked about the difference be-tween school and education, astutely told me what most students are already thinking, on some level:

> *"Education is about learning, where school is about passing, as in getting grades."*

A thirty-year old or a fifty-year old is more likely to overcome the pull of grades, and instead focus on the subject being studied and the process of learning. It's difficult, though, for a thirty or fifty year old to understand that younger students do not have this abil-ity to overcome structural conditions so easily. Elementary through college undergrad, students whose focus is shifted to the impor-tance of getting good grades have been strongly "motivated"—in the wrong way—pushed firmly into "completion mode." (By the way, it's no coincidence that graduate-level classes and programs have much less concern with grades.)

It is important to ask not just "how" to grade, but why we grade at all. A teacher of private guitar lessons does not "grade" their student. A parent does not "grade" their child when teaching them words at a young age. We do not "grade" each other when we are speaking to each other in normal conversations, outside of school, and showing each other new stuff. Grades, once again, are not about learning, but control. It can be argued that this control is necessary for learning, but this is a facile argument. You'll always find in these conversations that the negative effects of grades are dismissed or never brought up. Again, not a coincidence.

Alfie Kohn has summed up the research on grades from the 1980's and 90's. In his free online article, *The Case Against Grades*, he tells us that the research supports "three robust conclu-sions" about the negative effects of grading:

1. Grades tend to diminish students' interest in whatever they're learning.
2. Grades create a preference for the easiest possible task.
3. Grades tend to reduce the quality of students' thinking.

It's so strange to me that we as educators *definitely do not want* these things to happen to our students, and yet, many educators in my experience seem reluctant to spend a minute on considering that grades are inherently problematic, and perhaps even unnecessary.

Just because something has been done for a long time, and is done so pervasively, doesn't make it right. Right? Why are we so hesitant to criticize the idea of "grading" students? Especially when there is so much evidence and reason against it?

Again, I know why—in that I rationally understand the "reasons" people defend bad practices—but at the same time, I am still a bit baffled by the persistence of grades.

I have been watching and listening for so long in the schools, and all I hear and see is that grades are good; grades are necessary; grades are motivational. That's it. Never any questioning of them. Never any downside articulated. Just, sometimes, a conversation on how to do the wrong thing *differently.*

It is a conversation that totally misses the point. A major part of the point is that grades are powerful extrinsic motivators, and that is why we don't need more of it, but less of it. And ultimately, they need to go.

—

Now imagine again, the school system generalized as one person. There is poison coursing through this person's veins. Lots of different poisons—extrinsic motivators—the chief among them called grades. Our hypothetical person thinks this is not poison. These are vitamins and minerals. This is what the person needs to function.

It's not just poison, it's a parasite. The system is convinced that this is how it must work. But rather than de-grading, the system is slowly degrading. Students do not want to learn. They go to school for the certificate, and because it's the law. Teachers see the poison, and use the wrong antidote, often because they believe it's their only available option.

I would like for educators to name the poison and come up with a real antidote. Actually, finding the antidote is not necessary, because it's already found and we just need to take action in applying it more broadly. The antidote to the poison of extrinsically motivated students is not *more* extrinsic motivation, or, more poison. It is removing the extrinsic motivators, and replacing them with an intrinsically-motivating *environment*.

It is creating a school system that does not cure toxins by being more toxic, but, by identifying what is actually "nutritious"— an environment that is intrinsically motivational—so that students can engage more deeply with learning.

Chapter Six
Portraits Of Student Motivation

The extrinsically-motivated student

An extrinsic orientation tends to produce lower quality of learning, less interest in learning, less deep thinking, less sense of responsibility, less initiative, lack of direction, lack of focus, lack of purpose, and persistent misbehavior. This is what we could logically expect from students being forced into "completion mode," as if they are doing everything like it's filling out a job application. The students feel thoughtless, joyless, and pointless.

It's what we could expect from all the "motivators" framed as rewards, as in, you learn in order to get some other thingy; and "consequences," as in, you wouldn't want to learn if you weren't first threatened to do it.

The extrinsically-motivated student...

- Rarely talks about the stuff they're covering in class
- Seems to have a "bad attitude" about "learning"
- Must be constantly re-directed by the teacher, behaviorally and/or intellectually
- Must be "begged" by the teacher to do an assignment(s)
- Must be "enticed" by the teacher to do "more" and "better," with grades and other enticements
- Only learns material for the quiz or test
- Easily forgets the material, especially after the quiz or test is done.

- Only does something when it is for a grade
- Cannot explain much about the subject/content at the end of the course
- Will say that she doesn't like being in class
- Has a facial expression that is placid, aversive, and depressing (about class things, at least)
- Rarely raises his hand, answers questions, or asks questions
- Gives substitute teachers an extra hard time with behavior and "doing the work"
- Is easily distracted by guests entering the classroom
- Is easily distracted by anything and everything other than the assignment
- Talks about how he/she just wants to leave and/or graduate
- Cannot wait until school/class is over
- Uses language like "what's the point" and "why do I need this"
- Seems to care a lot about comparing and contrasting evaluations with other students, as if that's what matters most
- Makes the classroom seem like a constant battle-zone—or on the other end of the spectrum, a graveyard. Teacher feels like he/she is constantly dragging the students along and always having to "manage" them.

Of course, there are other factors that will affect the students, and even if a student is "extrinsically" motivated in a certain teacher's classroom, that is not all the fault of that particular teacher. But these are signs for teachers to notice and potentially adjust what they are doing. The goal is that the entire school (and eventually the entire school system) observes these signs as feedback of what it is doing—and then adjusts its own activity on the basis of that feedback. The main observation to make is that when someone is extrinsically motivated, they are not in "the zone" or "the flow"— and certainly not happy, and most likely, not fully engaged. The more we look with honest eyes, and the closer we look, the more it becomes clear.

The intrinsically-motivated student

Intrinsic motivation, as we can recall from an earlier list, has a lot to do with personal interest, joy, curiosity, engagement, and so on. It seems to me that there is some kind of inverse relationship between intrinsic and extrinsic motivation, just as there is some kind of inverse relationship between curiosity and compulsion. The intrinsically-motivated student might look something like this:

- Asks a lot of questions without being constantly prompted
- Adds own opinions/comments without being constantly prompted
- Takes initiative rather than waiting for instructions (or simply, "instruction")
- Goes beyond the minimum requirements, even if not tangibly "rewarded" for it
- Is not constantly trying to "game" the system and/or cut corners
- Does assignments that were not assigned
- Talks about the class content on his/her own time, in the lunchroom, at home, etc.
- Impresses substitute teachers and other classroom guests with how "focused" they are
- Is not so distracted by classroom guests, school announcements, or a bug on the floor
- Is gaining a clear depth of understanding that is beyond mere memorization
- Doesn't like leaving class or school

- Warm disposition, receptive attitude
- Joyful expressions, positive language
- Frequently makes connections with class material and the outside world
- Is not phased by high or low grades

Once again, this is not purely a reflection of individual teachers and their own classrooms. There are other factors. For example, students can like "math" and their math teacher, and everything that is happening in math class—and still be reserved when it comes to commenting and asking questions. This student might feel unsafe for other reasons, or simply be a quiet person. Another example of an externality would be the substitute teacher anecdote: there is some degree of "mob attitude" when it comes to substitute-teacher-day that may overwhelm a student's interest and initiative in class on that day. (Though the intrinsically-motivated student stands a much better chance of resisting this mob attitude.)

On the flip side, students may be well-behaved on "sub day" because they have been threatened with disciplinary consequences by the regular teacher, and/or the teacher made sure to leave an assignment that is worth a lot of "points," and so the students must dutifully get to work. (The students in this case may be well-behaved, but they are still being motivated "extrinsically.")

It is also true that students can acknowledge they need a good grade while pursuing that project out of interest. (Though it is less likely to become immersed in a project when it is for a grade.) The dilemma of an intrinsically-motivated student is that to remain intrinsically-motivated she must vigilantly keep the extrinsic elements at bay if she wants to pursue a project out of interest *and* receive a good evaluation. Students should not have to do this, and I believe the younger a student is, the less likely they are going to be able to consciously do this.

My list is a sketch, not a perfectly precise explanation of every circumstance or every student. And we can't always tell what is going on in the students' hearts and minds. These are simply signs for the teacher, parent, and others to observe in our attempt to understand how—not simply "how much"—students are motivated.

Not all "internal" motivation is "intrinsic"

I always keep in mind that students have been socialized, for thousands of hours, in school and their daily lives, to respond to certain things and not others. It is totally possible, though less likely, to be interested in learning something while only pursuing it *after yelled at*—when given a deadline, say, or when threatened with a high-stakes evaluation.

It is also possible, and I would say frequent, for students to *seem* intrinsically-motivated—while they are only doing the thing because they've been promised rewards or threatened with consequences.

The "intrinsic" student is doing the thing out of a deeply personal sense of wanting to do it. The student who has merely internalized "extrinsic" motivation, on the other hand, may do things on their own, but it is still an internal feeling of compulsion that drives them.

For an example, consider the employee who goes to work every day, is always on time, is very reliable, etc.—but doesn't necessarily enjoy it, and doesn't fully engage with the task.

Or consider the OCD tic of having to wash one's hands for five minutes. No one is telling this person to do so, and this person does not necessarily want to do so—but he does so—without instructions or prompting from someone else.

The student who has internalized the "extrinsic" pull of threats and bribes, punishments and rewards, carrots and sticks, may be very diligent and hardworking. This person may not need anyone to tell him/her to do things. But, this student is still not "intrinsically-motivated." This student is extrinsically-motivated, just less obviously, and perhaps more consistently.

The student who has systematically internalized "extrinsic motivation" might look like:

- Very hardworking, but miserable about it. Sometimes openly. Often, quietly.
- Doesn't need to be told to be quiet in order to be quiet—but doesn't necessarily enjoy being quiet.
- Gets good grades—but does not pursue much outside of the school/classroom. Doesn't seem curious, creative, or self-initiating, particularly when (or maybe only when) in the "extrinsic" environment.

It could also be thought of as an extrinsically-motivated student who is "self-regulated." This student is easy to instruct and easy to command. Often well-behaved, and seemingly a "good student"; but this student does not necessarily have intellectual curiosity or a strong sense of self-determination.

We don't want to create or contribute to this problem. Yes, it is a problem, even if it makes the students easier to deal with. I recall an article titled *"When is a good day of teaching a bad thing?"*, written by Timothy F. Slater, associate professor and education director at the University of Arizona.[26] Slater prompts the teacher: *have you ever had a good day?* A nice and easy day where the classroom was "manageable," most homework was turned in, the lesson plans were precisely-executed, and the students were quiet and participatory... in other words, a bad textbook's definition of a good day in the classroom. This describes what many administrators or politicians would want to see in a classroom: simple order.

Slater continues to pose questions throughout the article, and the questions can be summed up to this: are the students really learning much on these so-called "good days"?

Following instructions is not education. Even if the students seem to be happily doing it on their own, an orderly classroom does not mean quality learning is taking place. The extrinsically-motivated but "self-regulated" student is doing what seems to be a good job, but ultimately, they're doing it for the wrong reasons. They're doing it because they've been socially pressured. They're doing it to pass. And often they may be doing it because it's all they know they *can* do in school. Consequently, they are not learning very well. They are probably not learning the right things, and almost certainly they are not learning to love learning.

—

Learning to tell the difference is a continual process. But after understanding the fundamental concept, and looking for these signs in our daily lives, the difference becomes more clear. The difference between an extrinsically-motivated student and an intrinsically-motivated student is like the difference between a mercenary and a freedom fighter. It is, at least temporarily, a dim soul vs a bright spirit. It is wanting to be there versus not wanting to be there.

It is becoming mediocre at something—or maybe even "good" at something—versus acting on our innate curiosity, cultivating our potential, and becoming who we really can be.

It may become so clear to you as the difference between night and day. I hope so!

Chapter Seven
Switching Gears

A chapter on ridding extrinsic motivators from the school system could be a book of its own, because it will take so much thought and effort to create these different kind of classrooms, schools, and a new system from the ground up. So I'm just going to keep it short and simple.

If you want to stop seeing the bad stuff in chapter 6, stop doing the stuff in chapter 5. But that's where we start, not where we end.

And as we move away from "extrinsic" schools and classrooms, we build "intrinsic" schools and classrooms. I will be documenting my own journey on my blog: *https://teacherasguide.blog*.

This has to be a conversation, not a set of instructions from the writer to the reader, or from the superintendent or the principal's office, or just a set of mandates from capitol hill.

I think one of the most important steps in creating the schools we want is first understanding the concept of intrinsic and extrinsic motivation, not just referring to everything as "motivation."

In section three I have more suggestions to give, and more points from which to start a conversation.

Part III
Building the "intrinsic" environment

Chapter Eight
Student-centered Schools And Classrooms

"Instead [of extrinsic motivators], Deci and Ryan say we should focus our efforts on creating environments for our innate psychological needs to flourish."[27]

-Dan Pink

There is a lot in the concept of a "student-centered" education system, and I think it is one of the best points to start in the conversation of improving education. If we were to imagine a futuristic education system, one closer to our ideal, it would look like this concept of "student-centered" schools and classrooms.

The essence of the concept is implied in the term itself. We want education to be "centered" around individual students, and particular groups of students, who are living and learning in their specific circumstances.

This can be contrasted with "traditional education," in which "The center of gravity is outside the child"—as said by John Dewey one hundred years ago. There are other terms for this, like "teacher-centered"—or, since it's a system much larger than the teacher, I call it "institution-centered." On a scale, our system as it exists right now would lean pretty far to the "institution-centered" side. You know, maybe that's why we "need" so many extrinsic motivators. The system is not so concerned with the students' needs and interests, when it should be. Logically, the more we can bring school in line with their needs and interests, the less we would have to push and convince and coerce them.

If you are a teacher or someone else familiar with how schools are currently operating, think of what schools and classrooms look like, right now, within this framework. I pose a few questions to help:

- Who is making the curricular decisions?
- Who is making the students' schedules?
- Who is making the evaluations?
- Who is making the rules?
- Who is setting the standards?

Our answers to these questions will vary some, but there is a simple answer that gets straight to the point, and is undeniable: "*Not the students.*" In our present day schools and classrooms, the students make *very few decisions* about **what** they are learning; **when** they are learning; **how** they are learning; and even **why** they are learning.

From there, it shouldn't be so difficult to see why students are "de-motivated" and have such "bad attitudes." School is not about them in particular. It is largely *standardized*, with the goals and methods set by *institutions* and whoever is a part of those institutions. The institution includes teachers, administrators, policy makers, and so on; students generally are allowed just a small place in determining their own learning.

Then there is the question of who is "*doing*" the education. Are students *passive* or are they *active*? One huge misconception is that if students are doing "activities," that means they are being "active learners." While it is a step in the right direction for students to be doing activities, not just constantly being lectured at, activities alone do not make for active learners. That is because active learning has to do with the student thinking critically, deeply, enthusiastically, and in new ways. "Activities" alone do not guarantee any of that, especially when the activities are so often an exercise in step-by-step repetition, recitation, and regurgitation.

In classrooms where students are doing activities and projects —not simply sitting and listening—we would have to return to the question of who is making the choices. **Are students *driving their own learning*,** or are they mostly *following the teacher's instructions?*

A classroom that is "centered" around the learner would begin with that individual learner's (and/or group of learner's) interests, and work outward from there. If students don't know their interests, that speaks to a problem of their previous schooling experience (how it has diminished their curiosity, and not helped them discover their interests). We should take whatever opportunity we can to make schooling more an exploration of their own interests, and working outward from there toward new knowledge and ideas.

To some degree it is true that in school, students can pick from a limited amount of classes they might be interested in. But *within* these classes, there is often little room for students to learn what they are particularly interested in. In this way, we are less likely to activate their intrinsic motivation and greater learning power. Students who would like to learn on their own terms are especially out of luck in the commonly standardized classroom, whose goals are pre-fabricated before the students ever walk in the door on the first day of school. Even if they chose that class from a limited amount of possible courses, that does not mean their interests will be engaged.

Going back to the classroom of "activities," we could ask some questions: Did the students help shape the criteria on which they would be evaluated? If not, the student will be mainly following instructions, in order to ensure as good of an evaluation as possible. They will be in "completion mode."

Does the student have a say in deadlines? If not, it is difficult to maintain interest, and create and initiate on your own terms, when you are working on someone else's very specific timeline.

Does the student have a say in the topic, or at least the subtopic? If not, there is only so much a student can get hooked on something they don't care about. Even a great teacher, who can make an unfamiliar thing interesting, is swimming upstream if the students are not given much choice on the specifics of what is being studied, and *how* that thing is being studied.

These are some of the questions that, if answered, illustrate how our school system is largely centered around the "institution's" needs and wants, not the student's. It is true that sometimes the "institution's" needs and wants will overlap with the student's; it is also true that good teachers have some ability to accurately determine what certain students need and want. But the teacher does not and can not possibly know what is most relevant for all of the students. And if the *professional teacher* cannot know these things on their own, without activating the students to reflect and pursue their own interests in some way, you can imagine how much less *the people outside the classroom* would be able to pre-package a relevant education for them.

There is no such thing as a "relevant" education that is pre-packaged. That is a contradiction, like if I said I'm sitting while I'm also standing. If the students are left out of the learning decisions, it is not a "student-centered" school or classroom, no matter how much lip service is given by the institution. A standardized curriculum can not be relevant because students are not standard. A standardized evaluation criteria can not be such a thing as "fair," because every student has different lives and different goals, and often there is no absolute or agreed-upon truth by which to compare the student's work. The evaluations will pose as objective but actually will be subjective, and to many students this will seem intrusive and unfair. That's because generally speaking, it is.

The main point here is that students need to be empowered to build their own education, not just accept whatever is given to them and then follow through on it. There needs to be both a *school culture* that is student-centered, and *classrooms* that are student-centered.

Learner-centered Schools

Those who design, administer, and work in schools should spend a lot of time studying Deci and Ryan's *self-determination theory*. Within this theory, there are three elements that lead to someone becoming "self-determined," which essentially means that this person feels healthy, empowered, and intrinsically-motivated. The three elements are: 1. autonomy 2. relatedness 3. competence.

> "Conditions supporting the individual's experience of **autonomy, competence,** and **relatedness** are argued to foster the most volitional and high quality forms of motivation and engagement for activities, including enhanced performance, persistence, and creativity. In addition, SDT proposes that the degree to which any of these three psychological needs is unsupported or thwarted within a social context will have a robust detrimental impact on wellness in that setting."

> -Selfdeterminationtheory.org

Schools must be structurally designed to maintain and nurture (rather than disregard and destroy) the students' self-determination. I will now explore some of the implications of this principle for schools and the school system.

Autonomy

A good definition of autonomy is "freedom from external control or influence; independence." Oh boy, now consider the typical school, in which students are extremely controlled and essentially forced to be highly dependent on the adults. This nurtures nearly the opposite of a student who feels "autonomous."

We will have to change many school structures to give the students more freedom and independence. This might mean:

- Students are able to choose more of their classes.
- Students and classes are no longer necessarily on a rigid bell schedule.
- Students are encouraged to take responsibility, rather than simply follow instructions, which will mean students are given less "artificial" consequences for breaking rules, and instead, there is more focus on problem solving together, and re-directing the students' attention to the "natural" consequences of their actions (including, how their actions affect other people).
- Remember, both punishments and contingent rewards are devices of control. The more punishments and rewards, the less "autonomous" the students will feel. Extrinsic motivators should be removed as much as possible and whenever possible.
- Stop bossing students around in the hallways and offices. Notice how it doesn't work in the long-term? That's largely because it does not help the students feel autonomous, in fact, it makes them feel less in control of what they're doing and what they could do.
- Students should be brought into decisions on how the school is run, in significant ways. Be imaginative here.

- In schools of the near future, students are given more freedom in choosing when and where to be, *at least* during *some* of their school day. I will write about this elsewhere, but it would involve a re-design of the school day so that students can choose where to be during some of their day (library, gym, music room, for example...) and then can choose many of their classes during the other part of their day.

- There are many more solutions for supporting students' autonomy, please come up with your own.

Competence

Fostering a sense of competence would mean that we support and develop the students' sense that they are capable of meeting current challenges, and their life ahead. While educators certainly intend and wish to develop a sense of competence in their students—and in some ways, *do* succeed in this—in other ways, we systematically undermine the students' sense of competence.

Simply look at our system of grading, scoring, ranking, and praising in schools. "Success" is arbitrary and artificial; relative and conditional; with the "better" and "best" students achieving scarce awards and rewards for meeting whomever else's expectations.

Even the "successful" students have their sense of competence harmed. Why do you think? How can this be true? Well it's true because these successful students know that their success was conditional and continent, and it was not necessarily "success" at what they personally view as successful. They may have "succeeded" at something they do not find important, and only because they were so pressured into succeeding. Or maybe they got there by taking the easy classes, or simply having more helpful parents. Probably they know that they could fall at any time, and it's a much longer fall if you've been labeled as one of the "successful" ones.

To support and develop the students' sense of personal competence, our schools will require some fundamental changes. Here are some logical conclusions of applying self-determination theory to schools.

- Evaluation systems should not be about "relative" success, so that there is one winner and the rest are losers.
- Evaluations, including teacher-created tests and teacher-given grades, should not be high-stakes.
- Evaluations should not be done often. (Much less "all the time," like we are currently doing.)
- Educators should be more concerned with "feedback" and "problem solving" than with evaluation.
- Ranks and ratings generally should be abolished.
- Grades should be gradually diminished and then abolished.
- Educators should change their language so that they stop comparing the students to each other all the time. (more on this in chapter 10)
- Competition in the school environment should be minimal to none, instead, embracing cooperation and collaboration.
- Students should be brought into the process of creating their own evaluations, assignments, and learning goals.
- Think of your own; and pay attention to how students begin to see themselves after we say or do certain things. It would be a good idea to stop doing things that make them feel incompetent, even if those policies and practices are embedded in the school tradition. Prevalence does not make rightness. For building competence, what students need is unconditional support, not conditional judgments. What they need is a major say in setting their own goals and methods, not having all of it written out for them.
- Again… this is not a comprehensive list.

Helping the students feel competent doesn't mean we have to lie to them, or coddle them unnecessarily. It means finding ways to tell the truth without crippling their belief in themselves. The *truth* is that students are different from each other: they are not all going to succeed at the same things, in the same way, in the same time frame. Not only should that be fine, it should be expected. And who are the ones defining "success," anyway? Shouldn't *the students* be a part of that? Accomplishing goals that they helped to set in the first place, and being allowed to honestly reflect on their own strengths and weaknesses, is a good approach to helping students develop a true sense of competence.

Relatedness

Relatedness refers to "the universal want to interact, be connected to, and experience caring for others." This is a need and desire that humans seem to universally have, and it is very important for people to feel this way in their younger years of development, lest we form a belief in youth, that is difficult to shake off, that we cannot connect with others.

The feeling of relatedness is undoubtedly an aspect of someone's health. Better health also means better learning. I am a high school teacher, so I'm most familiar with extra large schools in which students transition every 45 or 50 minutes according to a bell schedule. Each teacher has between one hundred students (if they're lucky) and two hundred students (if they're a music teacher or something). These are divided into five or six different classes per day. This is ridiculous.

High schools are like an assembly line or a revolving door. It's difficult to form and maintain a sense of "relatedness" in this kind of impersonal environment. Where it does happen, it could happen much more often and more reliably if we changed how schools were structured.

I know it's difficult to believe, but in the United States of America in 2017, the standard high school gives students a few measly minutes between classes, often in large school buildings that require all of that transition time to get to the next class. Then, when students get to class, teachers are expected to have them paying attention from bell to bell. Students are being "instructed" by the teacher more often than not; in many classrooms, the students are not working collaboratively very much at all.

There's not much time in the school day for students to be casual, or intellectual, with their peers—much less to experience a whole-school sense of community.

Educators in these schools generally do their best to make lemonade out of lemons, but will never be able to mitigate the effects of schools that are too large and transient. It would be better to not be overwhelmed with so many lemons in the first place, than have to continue trying to make lemonade out of a never-ending supply of them. Anyways, some ideas for fostering a sense of community and belonging are:

- Schools should be much smaller than they are. A thousand students is still too much of a crowd for teenagers to feel like they belong. (Now think of the high schools that have two, three, or five thousand students.) Yes, some may do fine in this environment, but that is not the point. Many will *not* do fine in this environment. Don't we want *all* students, not just some of them, to feel that school is a place where they are included and cared about?

- Deb Meier and Ted Sizer, two profound education thinkers and practitioners in the 20th century, experimented with small schools and found that students, especially those coming from difficult home and community circumstances, do better in schools that number in the few hundred, not the few thousand. Deb Meier saw small schools as the way for students to develop meaningful relationships; an understanding of "democracy" in action; and a greater sense of responsibility among the students. The larger a school gets, the less likely students will learn these invaluable and immeasurable lessons.

- Class sizes should be smaller as well. One standing principle of Ted Sizer's Coalition of Essential Schools is that "efforts should be directed toward a goal that no teacher have direct responsibility for more than 80 students in the high school and middle school and no more than 20 in the elementary school." In these schools, teachers often have some responsibility for "non-instructional" roles, like counseling, which improves trust, community, and relatedness. (As well, teachers are "generalists first" in these schools, and specialize in a subject, second. In this way, the students are viewed and treated more holistically.)

- Ultimately, schools should move toward interdisciplinary study and away from the concept of students changing classes every hour by the sound of the bell in order to acquire a certain amount of "credits." (Ted Sizer called it "seat time.") More time should be spent in one or two homeroom classes and not split between eight teachers and rooms per day. Schedules should incorporate more "free time"—yes, *free time*—for students to spend longer lengths of time in a place of their choosing, like the gym, library, some teacher's homeroom, or even the lunch room. This will allow students to be around their most valued teachers, staff, and peers for a longer amount of time.

- Schools and individual teachers should have more "democratic" meetings (as opposed to the occasional assembly in the auditorium in which the students are simply expected to sit quietly and listen to the school rules or guest speaker). This will allow students to really work through problems, and communicate serious and not-as-serious issues.

- The school's mission should be more focused on fostering social and civic development—in actual structure and practice—*not just writing it in their mission statement.*

Of course, there are more solutions than the ones listed here. If educators begin to widely understand self-determination theory, how important it is, and what are its building blocks—I'm sure the profession will come up with more solutions than even my over-active imagination could imagine.

—

Schools that support and build self-determination already exist. Though they are largely outside the mainstream of the US public school system, there is no good reason it has to be that way. I recently discovered a long-time educator named Judy Yero who went on a journey around the country into various "learner-centered" schools. She wanted to personally experience and understand what differentiates learner-centered schools from traditional public schools. One thing she noticed is that "a learner-centered curriculum focuses on the holistic development of the individual child—the integration of the mental, physical, emotional, social, creative, spiritual, and natural domains of being human." [28]

Already, this "learner-centered" school is very different from the typical public school. Agree? The schools which I've attended, observed, and worked in, were heavily focused on "academics," and to some extent, sports and clubs. Or to put it another way, schools are typically focused on "facts and skills" much more than they are concerned with health and well-being; or the development of positive learning attitudes; or the nurturing of creative individuals; or the importance of community; or the complexities of living in a democratic society. Yes, schools do these things in the margins, and teachers try their best to promote these things when they can, but they are not a primary focus.

The problem is that all of these positive attributes are a part of what "education" is, or at least what it could be—but our schools, in practice, consider these other elements of a "holistic" education far less important than purely "academic" study.

It reminds me of how educators frequently say students are "off-track," but, who's really off track here? Considering that we do not show much concern, in practice, for the broader health and development of students, I would say it's the schools who are off track—and yes, the society in which the schools are rooted.

In learner-centered schools, the beliefs and expectations of educators are qualitatively different. That seems like a major first step in creating the right kind of schools.

> "While the methods and actual organization of the schools differed widely, their beliefs about children did not."[29]

> -Judy Yero

Judy found that some of the major factors or *necessary conditions* of these learner-centered schools were:

- Relationships
- Trust
- Self-directed learning
- Active, rather than passive, learning
- Self-reflection

While these traits are not totally absent from our mainstream public schools, and educators wish (and do their best) to bring these qualities into the learning environment in regular public schools, the mainstream schools are not *fundamentally built* around these concepts. Take "trust," for example. The default mode of educators and administrators in regular public schools is not one of trusting the students, rather, it is a *strong skepticism* of the student population. It is widely acknowledged and expected that the students will simply deviate without us. If we take our eye off them, they will break the rules. If we allow them to evaluate themselves, they will simply give themselves all A's. If we don't assign work, or outline the instructions precisely, they "won't know what to do." If we give them a "free day," all hell will break loose. Though educators do believe that their students have positive traits, and can do good things, there is a pervasive, fundamental cynicism about the students. I have been in thirty public high schools or so, and have not found one school environment that is an exception to what I just described.

There are other differences in learner-centered schools, as well, and Judy Yero identified some, like integrated learning and mixed-age learning. She noted that technology in the best "learner-centered" schools was simply a tool, not a replacement for teachers and other adult mentors. Again, these ideas can certainly be found in regular public schools—but in fragments, rather than being the very fabric of the school.

I highly recommend reading Judy's article on learner-centered schools (see previous citation). It is important to create school cultures that are much more caring and trusting of students, in general, and when it comes to how they are learning. It is important to create schools in which the students feel like it is a caring community—to the point that the people at school are like a second family (or a first family, for some).

Creating a learner-centered school, to some, may sound easy

or simple. But if that's the case, then why aren't we doing it? Good question. I really do hope people come to believe it's easy (it's often not) and it's simple (it can be). Let's get to work.

And to others, it will seem impossible to create schools like this. Just say to those people: don't get in the way of the people who are doing it. We don't need everyone to agree, to get to work.

I have a lot to say about school culture in my online writings, and will write more on this in the future. For now, I will move on and look at the student-centered classroom.

The student-centered classroom

Here's our current approach. The student walks into class on the first day of school. The teacher tells them what the class is about. The teacher tells them what will be studied. The teacher tells them the rules. The teacher tells them what every thing is "worth." The teacher tells them the "consequences" for failing to follow through. The teacher then creates and assigns all the lessons and assignments for the rest of the year. The students are mainly to sit back and do whatever is given to them. For best results, they will do it precisely to the teacher's specifications. It's as if education is as simple as following the steps to bake a cake.

But even baking a cake can be much more complicated than following instructions. Call our current schools teacher-centered, or institution-centered, or whatever you want, I guess, but reality is that our current approach is not centered around the students' needs and interests. A teacher who cares a whole lot about their students doesn't mean that classroom will automatically become a student-centered classroom. Even a brilliant teacher, who is surely better at understanding their own students than some politician is, will be limited in their ability to get the students *learning well* and *learning relevantly,* if the students are not solicited for their point of view and then consistently given opportunity to drive and define their own learning.

I hope I am making this clear: Education centered around the students' needs and interests is not only good philosophy, it is how science has determined thus far that people learn best. It is not a matter of mere opinion, like, which color is my favorite, red or blue. Active students learn better than passive students, period, and our school system has students in a very passive mode, which is an obvious observation if one were to honestly look around the schools.

People work and learn and live better in smaller communities of trust, and our schools can do a much better job of creating these sort of communities. There's really no disputing this.

Students who enjoy what they are doing—and are motivated *intrinsically*—develop better long-term attitudes about learning and greater well-being. Period.

If we're serious about education, and future generations, we've got a lot of work to do. And collectively, we have enough understanding about what we *need* to do.

Classrooms for flourishing

Alfie Kohn in his book *Punished by Rewards* identified "the three C's" to creating environments conducive to student well-being and intrinsic motivation.[30] These are:

- collaboration (or, community)
- content (or, curriculum)
- choice (or, autonomy)

Daniel Pink in his book *Drive* identifies three fundamental necessities for healthy and motivated people[31]:

- autonomy
- mastery
- purpose

Both Alfie Kohn's and Daniel Pink's three fundamental concepts are similar to, and overlap with, Deci and Ryan's three building blocks of self-determination, which I previously mentioned: autonomy, relatedness, and competence. Different words are being used between these experts, but they are saying stuff that is very similar. There are recurring elements that appear in healthy people, and motivated learners, and there are reliable ways for creating the conditions which lead to healthy people and motivated learners.

For simplicity's sake, I will re-interpret Dan Pink's "autonomy, mastery, and purpose" into my own implications for creating a student-centered classroom. The end goal in this kind of classroom is for the means and ends to be geared toward students who become healthy and motivated, and who learn to love learning—and then, who *do* learn for real.

Autonomy

If any element for healthy and motivated learners is the most important, it would have to be "autonomy." In fact, I've seen this explicitly stated by Kohn, Pink, and Deci and Ryan. School environments must preserve and nurture the students' sense of autonomy — and so must the classrooms, where most learning is supposed to take place. Some implications for teachers on the importance of "autonomy" are:

- Classroom rules and procedures should be determined with, not simply for, the students in that classroom. The final policies should reflect a giving up of some of the teacher's control over the classroom, with regard to what the students are doing, and how, when, and why. The classroom must become "ours"—not simply "the teacher's."
- Curriculum and evaluations, as well, should be determined *with*—not simply *for*—the students. If someone wanted more specifics on precisely how to do this, searching the web would help, and I'll be writing more on my blog.

- Lessons and assignments should allow space for students to determine—again—what, when, and how. For example, a history teacher may be teaching on *World War II*. The students should not all have to study the same aspect of that war, when there is a near-endless amount to explore and learn within that one topic. Often, the teacher (and by implication, the evaluation criteria) should not expect all the students to give the "same answer." (*Of course*, this does not mean it is off-limits for the teacher to correct responses that are factually wrong. It means that much of what is studied should not simply have one correct answer, and often, the process of coming to an answer is as important as the final answer.) The teacher should give individuals and/or student groups some latitude in which part of the topic to explore, and *how* to present what they learned —whether it's a paper, presentation, skit, or whatever. Students will also learn a whole lot more this way, because many groups can be doing different things, and then will be presenting different stuff to their peers.
- (Give the students some choice in determining who will be a part of their group, and/or if they want to work alone.)
- Create deadlines with, not simply for, the students.
- Do not constantly evaluate the students during the learning process, which imposes on their ability to think and act freely, and gets them focused more on the evaluation than the learning (putting them into completion mode).
- Let the students evaluate themselves at the end of a unit or quarter/semester, and have that evaluation be part or all of their final "grade," if grades must be given. Again, there are many people who have written about this sort of thing, and I will be writing more on this process in the future.

Mastery

Mastery is similar to Deci/Ryan's "competence." People not only want to feel a significant degree of freedom while they work, learn, and live, but also to make accomplishments, and feel the joy that is inherent in challenge and improvement. Here are some ideas, for teachers, for allowing and promoting a sense of mastery:

- Bring students in on determining what their goals should be, and how they might get there. Not all students should have the same goals, or even the same way of getting there, because that would necessarily end with some students feeling incompetent. (Think of different animals being asked to climb a tree in the forest for their final exam, which is essentially what we are doing when we ask students to meet the same goals and standards on the same timeframe.)

- Have students reflect, occasionally, not constantly, on what they've learned and what they want to learn. The course content and direction should be influenced by these reflections.

- Have students make projects and build portfolios, that show—much more than tests and worksheets do—a tangible product that was created, or specific skill that was accomplished.

- Work to minimize and eventually abandon ranks and ratings (grades). For the "high achievers," good grades and scores will make them feel that their "mastery" is contingent on fleeting tasks and other peoples' evaluations. This is not a true sense of mastery. For the "low achievers," consistently poor ranks and ratings will make them feel like they are unable to master anything. They will feel this way despite that ranks and ratings in school are not "objective" evaluations of one's character and accomplishments, but subjective evaluations of one's success at the game of school. In other words, students who get poor grades and scores can truly, honestly master certain things in life, but will not realize this truth about themselves very well if they are getting bad grades and low scores.

- The teacher should acknowledge that he/she is not the only one who can, or should, teach the students. The teacher should then make more space for students to teach and learn from each other. Not only will the students be learning and mastering, they'll see that they can successfully teach others!

- Teachers can acknowledge when a student has truly taught *them* something. This will help the student feel an honest sense of being good at something, even if it's just that one idea.

- Teachers should downplay and move away from evaluation, and more toward reflective assessment (which is more potent for helping students learn and build their skills/knowledge, and has less destructive potential than evaluation).

- Teachers can also call or email parents to let them know when a student has done something significant. I know many teachers know this, and do it, but some don't, or it's easy to forget...

- Educators can generally use strategies that will build intrinsic motivation and enthusiasm for a subject, rather than undermine it. Intrinsic motivation and enthusiasm lead naturally to mastery.

Purpose

Purpose is like a mix of community, competence, and relatedness. One can be good at something, like painting or guitar, and still not feel a greater sense of purpose. The best way to promote a sense of purpose is to increase the sense of *relevance* to the greater whole, and build connectedness among a group and broader community. Students should see themselves as a legitimate part of the larger picture.

- Educators should be deliberate in connecting their subject and curriculum to careers, hobbies, and interests that exist outside of school. (If study gets too abstract, it will be difficult to defend the practicality and purpose of a certain thing. Abstract theoretical study is better for college and beyond, which is one reason interdisciplinary study is such a good idea for K-12.)

- Allow students to learn and work together, often, so they feel connected rather than isolated.

- Implement classroom meetings and decision-making among the students.

- Adults should treat high school students more like young adults, and less like little kids. Middle school students should be allowed to make more decisions than a 5-year-old would, etc.

- Incorporating social justice themes and topics into classroom study, with the results of "helping others" made more apparent. The outcomes of social justice on people within the community, and beyond the community, can be made clear. This is as opposed to what we seem to do now, which is simply giving rewards or credits to individual students upon task completion (see: service learning hours, etc.) Again, social justice and community service takes place around the margins of mainstream schools and classrooms, not as a fundamental part of them. That should be changed...

- Provide opportunities for students to learn outside the classroom—field trips, community events, and so on.

Combine with social justice, etc.

- Bring in guest speakers and various skilled practitioners from the field.
- Have students reflect on the positive results, to themselves and the community, of whatever they're learning/doing!

A long way to go

If the students are not determining much of what, how, and when to study, then it's not student-centered. If the point values are set, and the evaluations high-stakes, and only made only by others, it's not student-centered.

If the schools and classrooms are not student-centered, the students are not going to be so intrinsically-motivated. Their engagement is going to be limited. Their attitudes and well-being will suffer. They will not learn very well; they will not learn the right things that will be useful or interesting in the context of their own lives.

Despite the occasional teacher who is brilliant and inspirational, the students will systematically develop bad habits of mind, like, "learning is only a means to a very limited end—the acquisition of rewards or the avoidance of punishments." And, they will not develop their potential nearly as much as they could have.

This book is supposed to be more of a conversation starter than a conversation ender. I trust in educators enough that, once the right questions are raised, we can solve the problems together — not just take the answers from one book or one person. Better than answers are solutions, anyways, and solutions for us in the education field will necessarily be dynamic. They will be found over time, through research, continuous practice, dialogue, and experimentation.

I illustrated how our schools and classrooms are not student-centered, and why they should be. I gave some principles and strategies for creating a more student-centered education system. Now, it's up to the reader, and those around the reader, to think and imagine how things could be different in one's own circumstance. And then, how we could implement fair and practical solutions— to the problems that, hopefully, now, are more clear.

Chapter nine
Addressing Social And Political Failures

It would be a major mistake for teachers to think that if we just got the politicians off our backs, and funded public schools more fully, then students will suddenly be motivated and they will enjoy school and all will be dandy. Well, that would certainly help, but it would not substitute for a new conception of teaching and learning (built on a better understanding of motivation).

The reverse is only partly true, as well. Some believe that if teachers just knew or did the right thing, the United States of America would skyrocket to the top of the world education rankings, and all the students would get big brains and good jobs.

For argument's sake, let's say we did improve the teacher force, whatever that may mean. Let's say we did "fix" teacher education programs, again, whatever that might entail. Let's even imagine that educators suddenly and widely understood that extrinsic motivators have a strong tendency to undermine intrinsic motivation, and then began to put forward many radical solutions that follow from the implications of this new understanding of motivation.

Well, we'd still have lots of poor and sick students coming to school.[32] We'd still have students who learn certain ideas and habits from parents, peers, and pop culture—many of which are probably not so healthy or conducive to better quality learning.[33]

We'd still have schools that, in the United States, were funded by property tax, meaning rich kids would get rich schools and poor kids would get poor schools. [34] We'd still experience the issues that arise from a culture with a dogmatic belief in competition: a normalization of conflict, winning at whatever cost, and the idea that keeping each other down is not only okay, but often necessary for "success."[35]

We'd still be living in a country with high income-and-wealth-inequality, and a barbaric for-profit healthcare system which leaves many of us ill.[36] We'd still be living in a country where attending college is a sentence to decades of debt.[37] We'd still be living in a country where many parents of school students are unemployed, or must work two or three jobs to pay their modest bills.

We'd still be living in a society where some students' close friend was shot and killed by a gang member, or the police.

I could go on, but that's not necessary. The point is that teachers can only do so much, and in some ways, they are already doing too much. We are a sick society,[38] and it's best to admit it. I really wish it weren't so.

Here is a strong suggestion to teachers, and everyone else who wants to make a positive difference. Get political, and I don't just mean vote. Voting is not enough. Being political is much more than that. Educators should work to educate and organize outside the classroom. Everyone who cares about education, and the next generation, should be an activist.

To be a citizen should mean to be an activist, anyway. That's how democracy is supposed to work. If we don't like what society has become, well, it can only continue if all of us allow it to continue.

I like to respond to anyone who thinks badly of the education system that perhaps they are right. But I also like to add that the real problems are largely different than what is articulated in the mainstream narrative, and the problems, even in the education realm, will not be fixed solely by those in schools and classrooms.

To believe so would be incredibly naive.

Public education is a noble idea, and it can become something far greater than what it is now. To see the dream achieved, we need a greater vision—one that is not just a dream, but something that is possible through collective effort.

Then, we have to make it happen. Waiting around for cynical people in power to make the right changes for us—well, that's not going to happen. It's up to us.

Chapter ten
Learning A New Language (of Motivation)

"You must unlearn what you have learned."

-Master Yoda

"If you don't do the assignment, you'll lose points."
"If you misbehave, you'll get in trouble."
"Don't you want an 'A'?"

Carved into the language of educators is a flawed understanding of motivation. We ask and demand of students to think and act in ways that are ultimately demotivational. And much of what we're doing in schools is simply geared toward student compliance, at the expense of learning and loving learning. It would be prudent to ask why this is so, and how it could change. It would be nice for us to not confuse compliance with motivation.

There are choices we have to make. We can do it the easy way, and the way it's been done. Or, we can work to change the system.

The first way, though endlessly frustrating, is easier, no doubt. The other way, a commitment to change the system, is an attempt to fix the actual problem. The root problem is a system that, supposedly, requires extrinsic motivators in order to function—which essentially is an admission that the system is broken.

It is better to commit to solving a problem, and being part of the system change, than giving up and perpetuating what is so wrong. I believe that once we understand this new paradigm of motivation—that intrinsic and extrinsic motivation are different, and that they work in opposition—we will begin to see how harmful our policies, practices, and interactions are to the students' intrinsic motivation. Then, as educators, we can help each other continue to learn and grow—so that our students can—in the right ways.

It will require no less than learning a new language. But this new language will not be so unfamiliar. It reads like a list of reasons why teachers go into teaching—and the feelings people have when they love to learn.

For a reminder on the concept, you can always re-visit chapter two; chapter six; chapter eight.

Then, very important is to phase out the other language—the one of extrinsic motivation—so that it doesn't replace our new one. The "new" one is closer to home, anyways, and it's worth learning again.

Conclusion

Being Fair, Learning For Real, And Loving What We Do

If we acknowledge some better truths about human motivation, and take those better truths more seriously, there we'd find some major implications for classrooms and the education system.

Support vs Demand

I must once again credit Alfie Kohn for introducing me to so many significant concepts. In one online article, *"Grading: The question is not how, but why?"*, Kohn briefly describes two different paradigms of schooling. One could be called the "support" model, in which we support the students' intrinsic curiosity and offer them carefully crafted environments, and relevant lessons, to get them exploring ideas and loving learning. This is opposed to the "demand" model—our traditional (and modern) model—in which the students' goal is to conform to whatever the system demands of them. This is accomplished through the force of controlling mechanisms, punishments and rewards, carrots and sticks, inducements and incentives, extrinsic motivators.

Another way of describing essentially the same thing, Kohn frequently refers to a "working with" versus "doing to" paradigm. Or, we could call it "learner-centered" versus "institution-centered." We could say that we want an education system built around intrinsic motivation, rather than extrinsic motivation. We could begin to believe that the role of the teacher, and the institution, is not merely to "instruct," but more profoundly, to "guide." This is all part of the new language, and a renewed set of goals!

Educator Traits

It is not "easy" to change such a large system, the education system, and it can not be done by oneself. When I write it like that, it may sound obvious, but sometimes we begin to believe, when the going gets tough, that it should be easy—or that we can do it all in our own classroom. These are normal feelings, fine, but it's important to remind ourselves that it's not easy, and in some way it will require a broad effort. Despite this, it is worth it.

I am walking this road already, and I know some of what it will take to keep going. Educators, parents, and teachers in particular will need to develop some traits that they probably already have, but maybe not in great enough amounts if they want to fight this fight and transform the system.

Empathy

It will take even greater empathy than most teachers already have. Teachers will have to constantly think and feel how the students are thinking and feeling, and this will help to keep things in perspective when things don't seem to work out.

Integrity

It's difficult to keep an open mind to better ideas while also sticking to what you believe is best. But it is like a skill that can improve with time and effort. When we do figure out with strong certainty that something is good—and we honestly compare that with lesser options—we should stick with the better one, even despite the peer pressure and persistent traditions around us. It will take some creativity and resourcefulness to implement solutions in ways that are acceptable within the current system, but simultaneously effective in the ways we want them to be. Being effective in the better way will often mean doing it "wrong" as viewed from the old perspective. Minimizing the salience of grades, and, may the fates be with you, eliminating grades—will not initially be seen by most people as a "good" thing. Thoroughly prepared responses to the expected criticisms, and a skillful execution of the new plan, will help stay the path.

Research
What will help to keep one's integrity is being familiar with scientific research in the field, even research that is not popular, like the research showing that grades and other extrinsic motivators are demotivational. Reading this book is cool, but a mentality must be taken that is continuously devoted to analyzing findings in educational and social sciences. Educators should not completely abdicate their personal judgment, of course, but judgment must be informed by more than one's own personal experience. We must give serious consideration to research in the field.

And it doesn't necessarily have to be "scientific" research. There are teachers, parents, students, and schools reporting from all corners of the earth about some of the better ways of doing school. Sensibility and rationality should not be abandoned, nor should anecdotes. These should simply be tempered with formal research. Above all is to be honest, critical thinkers.

Patience
Finally, and perhaps what is most needed, is the ability to make it through difficult times and trust that the process is not quick. I can say that if I didn't have lots of patience, especially for my students, I probably would have quit by now. And I have not had a long-term teaching post yet. There's still no guarantee I will continue in

the profession, but, I think having patience can only help.

Without patience, we *will* give up. We will only look at short-term results: what happened today in the classroom; how the administration rated us this year; how some other teachers didn't seem to want to change very much; how so many people just don't get it (motivation); and how this year's politicians and their policies are garbage.

Again, it comes back to doing the right thing. That usually helps me, anyways.

Agitate, Educate, Organize

...is what it means to be political. This is how to grow the ranks. This is how we change the system. In the classroom, and out of it, we shake things up, in sensible and informed and humane ways, and we draw people to our truth and action. Some things will have to be done on one's own, but not everything can be. I've been putting lots of thought into which stuff can or must be done on my own, and which stuff can't.

Beyond Engagement

We want engagement, sure, but eventually I came to the belief that engagement is not the ultimate goal we seek as educators. It's simply not good enough, not guiding enough. In the idea of "engagement" there is not enough room to re-examine what we are asking the students to do, and why. There is an easy assumption in "engagement" that if we get students working, and following our instructions—and repeating back what we want to hear or see—that is all that needs to happen. That is our job as teachers, and that, we might think, is education.

Better than engagement is empowerment. After all, students can be "engaged," but not learning the right things or in the right way. It's more difficult to get "empowerment" wrong. A truly empowered student is one who is healthy and *intrinsically* motivated.

To be healthy and intrinsically motivated will arise out of the right environment, in which we help students be what they want to be—and what they need to be—and beyond. They will surprise themselves, and they will surprise us. Because humans are great without, in fact, despite, the dang carrots and sticks.

1   Alfie Kohn, "Why Lots of Love (or Motivation) Isn't Enough," alfiekohn.org, April 23, 2016

2   Alfie Kohn, *Schooling Beyond Measure* (Heinemann Publishing, 2015), p. 94.

3   Pasi Sahlberg, *Finnish Lessons 2.0* (Teachers College Press, 2015), p. 201.

4   Pasi Sahlberg, *Finnish Lessons 2.0* (Teachers College Press, 2015), chapter 5.

5   An OECD study, "Child income poverty rates, 2013 or nearest available year," shows ~20% child poverty in the United States versus ~5% in Finland.

6   Quote attributed to Paulo Freire, though I am not aware of the original source.

7   Alfie Kohn, "The Progressive Schools Our Children Deserve," alfiekohn.org, Fall 2005

8   Excerpt from an address by Albert Einstein to the State University of New York at Albany, October 1931.

9   Daniel Pink, *Drive* (Riverhead Books, 2011), p. 1.

10   Alfie Kohn, *Punished by Rewards* (Houghton Mifflin Harcourt, 1993), p. 43.

11   Ibid.

12   Ibid, p. 44.

13   Ibid.

14   Ibid.

15   Ibid, p. 47.

16   Original source material unknown. Quote was found in several places on the internet (but you know what Abraham Lincoln said about random quotes on the internet....) It's likely someone else said this, not Einstein, but the concept does fit

into what Einstein was saying in his earlier-cited speech.) He did make these observations even if he did not ultimately use these exact words.

17   Sarah S. Pak, "The Effect of Mandatory Reading Logs on Children's Motivation to Read." *Journal of Research in Education*, Volume 22, Number 1.

18   Alfie Kohn, *Punished by Rewards* (Houghton Mifflin Harcourt, 1993), p. 150.

19   Ibid.

20   Ibid.

21   Ibid.

22   Quote from Alfie Kohn, "No Grades + No Homework = Better Learning" DVD, Dellaruth Videos, 2009.

23   Alfie Kohn, *Punished by Rewards* (Houghton Mifflin Harcourt, 1993), p. 87.

24   Daniel Pink, *Drive* (Riverhead Books, 2011), p. 9.

25   Ibid, p. 70

26   Timothy F. Slater, "When is a good day of teaching a bad thing?", *The Physics Teacher, Vol. 41*, October 2003.

27   Daniel Pink, *Drive* (Riverhead Books, 2011), p. 70.

28   Judy Yero, "Common Factors in Effective Learner-Centered Schools," learninginmind.com.

29   Ibid.

30   Alfie Kohn, *Punished by Rewards* (Houghton Mifflin Harcourt, 1993), p. 213.

31   Daniel Pink, *Drive* (Riverhead Books, 2011), Part Two, "The Three Elements."

32   I recommend to search the web for studies on child poverty in public schools, and physical and mental illness.

33   If students are taught outside the school that learning is not valued, and certain other things are, well, that's the attitude they will bring into schools, creating yet another obstacle for teachers to help them learn certain things, or in general.

34   Recommend an article in *The Atlantic* by Alana Semuels, "Good School, Rich School; Bad School, Poor School." August 2016.

35   The book *No Contest* (Houghton Mifflin, 1986 / 1992) by Alfie Kohn is an examination of "competition" and its effect on our social health and individual well-being. Summary: overall, it's not positive like we tend to assume, and it's often negative.

36   Search the web for studies on wealth inequality

37   Check out a short YouTube video titled "Wealth Inequality in America." Wealth inequality in the United States is as high as it's been since the Gilded Age. Also, we are one of the few countries with a for-profit healthcare system, which empirically leads to higher costs, more untreated illness, and worse outcomes.

38   Recommend a report, "America's State of Mind," on the epidemic of mental illness in US society. Can be accessed through a google search.

About the Author

Sammy Kayes is a teacher and musician in Chicago, Illinois, and apparently now an activist and writer. His next book in this series will be a debunking of the "grading" practice/ideology. Follow his education blog at <u>teacherasguide.wordpress.com</u>.

www.ingramcontent.com/pod-product-compliance
Lightning Source LLC
Chambersburg PA
CBHW061739020426
42331CB00006B/1297